TYNEHAM
Dorset's Ghost Village
RODNEY LEGG

Tyneham House, drawn
by Alfred Dawson in
1882.

dpc
Dorset Publishing Company
at the Wincanton Press, National School, North Street, Wincanton, Somerset BA9 9AT

To the memory of **Mavis Caver**, **Monica Hutchings** and **Margaret Kraft**, and reliving exploits with **Barry Cuff**, **Marjorie Hillman**, **Ian Jures**, **Michael Key**, **John Pentney** and **Bill Strong** — who saved the Tyneham remains that you can now visit and enjoy.

Looking east along the Purbeck coast to Flower's Barrow, Gad Cliff and Worbarrow Tout, drawn by Alfred Dawson from the Arish Mell valley, 1882.

Source: Rodney Legg collection

Publishing details. First published 1992. Copyright Rodney Legg © 1992. All rights reserved. No part of this publication may be reproduced in any form or by any means, electronic, computerised, mechanical, photo-copying, recording or otherwise, without prior permission in writing from the publisher.

Printing credits. Typesetting input by Reg Ward at Holwell, Dorset, and output by Wordstream Limited, St. Aldhelm's Road, Poole. Printed by The Fairwood Press at Westbury, Wiltshire (telephone 0373 822044).

Distribution. Orders by post serviced by Dorset Publishing Company from the Wincanton Press, National School, North Street, Wincanton, Somerset BA9 9AT (telephone 0963 32583). Local distribution, to shops in the Dorset area, is undertaken for Dorset Publishing Company by Maurice Hann from 36 Langdon Road, Parkstone, Poole, Dorset BH14 9EH (telephone 0202 738248).

International standard book number. ISBN 0 948699 30 2

Map of western Purbeck: produced by F.S. Weller and W.H. Everett and Son in 1890. The tank firing ranges of the Royal Armoured Corps now extend along the coast from Lulworth Cove in the west to Kimmeridge Bay in the east (given here as 'Kimeridge'; watch the spellings). Inland, the Army lands stretch to Coombe Heath, Highwood Heath and along Holme Lane towards East Holme and the appropriately named Battle Plain. The eastern boundary is southwards from there – to Bridewell, Little Wood, Steeple Leaze Wood, Lower Stonehips and Charnel.

Source: Rodney Legg collection

Scale of English Miles

SOUTHERN COMMAND

TRAINING AREA, EAST HOLME, Nr. LULWORTH

IN order to give our troops the fullest opportunity to perfect their training in the use of modern weapons of war, the Army must have an area of land particularly suited to their special needs and in which they can use live shells. For this reason you will realise the chosen area must be cleared of all civilians.

The most careful search has been made to find an area suitable for the Army's purpose and which, at the same time, will involve the smallest number of persons and property. The area decided on, after the most careful study and consultation between all the Government Authorities concerned, lies roughly inside of the square formed by EAST LULWORTH—EAST STOKE—EAST HOLME—KIMMERIDGE BAY. *Including your properties – see overleaf.*

It is regretted that, in the National Interest, it is necessary to move you from your homes, and everything possible will be done to help you, both by payment of compensation, and by finding other accommodation for you if you are unable to do so yourself.

The date on which the Military will take over this area is the 19th December next, and all civilians must be out of the area by that date.

A special office will be opened at Westport House, WAREHAM, on Wednesday the 17th November, and you will be able to get advice between the hours of 10 a.m. and 7 p.m., from there on your personal problems and difficulties. Any letters should be sent to that address also for the present.

The Government appreciate that this is no small sacrifice which you are asked to make, but they are sure that you will give this further help towards winning the war with a good heart.

C. H. MILLER,
Major-General i/c Administration,
Southern Command.

16th November, 1943.

S.C.P. 24. 400. 11/43 S.P. 92944

TYNEHAM and EAST HOLME PARISHES

Above: Requisition notices were issued for military occupation of the entire 3,003 acres of the parish of Tyneham, plus extensive heathland parts of the adjoining parish of East Holme, and adjacent areas in the parishes of East Lulworth, East Stoke and Steeple. They were signed by Major-General Charles Harvey Miller [1894-1974] of Southern Command who was based at Wilton House, near Salisbury. The extension of the Armoured Fighting Vehicles School gunnery ranges, eastwards from Bindon Hill, Lulworth, was principally for training the crews of Sherman tanks – these currently being carried across the Atlantic in their hundreds and being unloaded in the South Wales ports. The area to be evacuated, without any mention of this in the newspapers, covered ten square miles. The whole of Dorset was already becoming an armed camp. Successions of special trains, called 'Warflats' from their special flat-bed wagons, brought the tanks and other armoured fighting vehicles to the coastal hinterland of south Dorset. The main force gathering in Dorset was the 2nd United States Armo[u]red Division of V US Corps of the First US Army, which would sail to Normandy as beach-heads were secured in the invasion of Europe which started in the early hours of 6 June 1944. The eviction notice is dated 16 November 1943.

Source: Rodney Legg collection

MUPE ROCKS

Looking east over Mupe Rocks to Flower's Barrow and Worbarrow Tout.

Photograph: Colin Graham

Phillip Brannon's engraving of Mupe Rocks, from the sea about 1860, showing Slip Rock, Arish Rock, Bacon House (on clifftop) and Hole, Wreckneck Rock and Bindon Hill.

Source: Rodney Legg collection

Worbarrow Bay

ARISH MELL GAP

From the sea (above),
in a Victorian print;
from the east with
Cockpit Head behind
(below) and wrecked
steam-boat about 1905;
and from the west with
a cow and car on the
beach, 1938.

Source: Rodney Legg collection
Snapshot courtesy: G. Atkins

AND WORBARROW BAY

Above: **From the slopes of Gad Cliff showing the chalk cliffs at Arish Mell Gap rising to the summit of Flower's Barrow hill-fort (top right). In the middle distance is the hamlet of Worbarrow with its cottages in the gullies and two modern away-from-it-all dwellings poised on the cliffs, namely the stone-built Sheepleaze and the brick Bungalow above it. About 1930.** Photograph: E. V. Tanner

Below: **The bay from the 1940 pillbox at the east end of Flower's Barrow, with Worbarrow Tout jutting out to sea, 1978.** Photograph: Rodney Legg

Worbarrow Tout and Hambury Tout, on the west side of Lulworth Cove, preserve an early hill-name, William Lisle Bowles observed in his 1828 'Dissertation on the Celtic Deity Teutates' – "most of the hills of the sea-coast, and through Dorsetshire, are still pronounced Teuts [Toots] by the common people."

DISCARDED CHURCHILL TANK, ON THE SLOPES OVERLOOKING WORBARROW BAY

Below: **Rusting war relic, used as a target, 1972.** Photograph: Rodney Legg

WORBARROW BAY

Previous double page spread:
Shipwreck in Worbarrow Bay, in a dramatic print with heaving sea by marine painter Clarkson Stanfield [1793-1867]; engraved about 1830. The scene is depicted from the beach, nearly half a mile north-west of the fishing hamlet of Worbarrow. Looking towards Worbarrow (left) with chimney smoke being blown almost horizontally from the south-west and the craggy 45-degree slope of Gold Down rising behind. Behind the wreck (centre) is the conical outline of Worbarrow Tout.
Print: Rodney Legg collection

Right: **The slope of Flower's Barrow (bottom left) and the view south-south-east, across Worbarrow Bay to Gad Cliff (left) and Worbarrow Tout (centre) with Kimmeridge Bay beyond and the profile of the inland headland of Swyre Head (centre horizon) dropping down to the southern tip of the Isle of Purbeck at St Alban's Head (far right). 1967.**
Photograph: Monica Hutchings

SEA COTTAGE, WORBARROW

Above: **Sea Cottage, beside the beach at Worbarrow Bay, was the home of the Miller family of fishermen. They had worked the lobster pots for generations. Thomas and Jack, the sons of Henry Miller, were to be the last of the line at Worbarrow. Their home is seen from the south-east, with an up-turned rowing boat in the foreground and the 550-foot cliff of Flower's Barrow hill-fort rising behind. The two-tone undercliff changes from multi-colour purple, red and yellow of Wealden bed sands to the white chalk of the Purbeck Hills. In the foreground (left and right) are the roofs of the two boathouses, one being for the use of the fishermen and the other used by the Bond estate. The landward gable of the right-hand boathouse is seen in the top picture overleaf. 1938.**
Photograph: Geraldine Paul

WORBARROW BAY

Opposite: **The western sweep of Worbarrow Bay, seen from the rusting 1940 anti-invasion wire on Worbarrow Tout. Looking across to Mupe Rocks (far left), Cockpit Head and the east end of Bindon Hill (centre), and the break in the chalk cliffs at Arish Mell Gap (towards the right). From the east. 1967.**
Photograph: Monica Hutchings

SEA COTTAGE, WORBARROW

Top: **From the east with Arish Mell Gap in the centre background, 1943.** US Army photograph

Right: **From the south-east, with picnickers Gladys Legg (the author's mother) and Arthur and Effie Pitman, about 1929.** Photograph: Ted Legg

Below: **From the south-west, across the beach, backdrop to an Edwardian trip around the bay, about 1906.** Photograph: Dorset County Museum

Opposite top: **From the south-west. 1940 anti-invasion wire in foreground, 1943.** US Army photograph

Opposite inset: **From the south-east, in 1969.** Photograph: Rodney Legg

Opposite bottom: **From the north-west, in 1969.** Photograph: Rodney Legg

COTTAGE ABOVE THE GWYLE, WORBARROW

Below top: **From the east, 1943. This was the home of Beattie and Winnie Mintern. Their smallholding supplied the valley with milk, butter and eggs. The butter-making was carried on in the thatched end of the house.**

Below centre: **From the north-west, with the Gwyle behind and the slopes of Gad Cliff beyond, 1943.**

Bottom: **From the south, 1943.** US Army photographs

COASTGUARD STATION, WORBARROW
later called HILL COTTAGE

Opposite top: **From the south-east with Arish Mell Gap behind the centre chimney, 1943. It was the home of Tom Miller, and before that his father, Henry Miller.**

US Army photograph

Opposite bottom: **From the north-east with Worbarrow Tout in the background and 1940 anti-invasion wire in the righthand foreground, 1943.** US Army photograph

Above: **The view from the south-east in 1970.**

Photograph: Rodney Legg

Below: **The view from the north-east in 1970.**

Photograph: Rodney Legg

COTTAGE, 50 FEET INLAND FROM THE BUNGALOW, WORBARROW

Above main picture: **From the north-east, 1943.**
Inset: **From the south, 1943.**
US Army photographs

FERN HOLLOW, 70 YARDS INLAND FROM SHEEPLEAZE, WORBARROW

Above: **From the east, with Sheepleaze above, 1943. It stood by the stream and was the home of Charles and Harriette Miller.**
US Army photograph

ROSE COTTAGE, WORBARROW

Above: **From the north-west, 1943. Arthur Stockley and his family lived here. It stood to the east of the one above, on the opposite side of the Gwyle stream from the Minterns' cottage pictured on the previous page.**

Below: **From the east (the cottage at the top of the page is glimpsed on the left side), 1943.**
US Army photographs

SHEEPLEAZE, WORBARROW

Above: **From the north, 1943.**
Below: **From the south-west. This 1920s holiday cottage on the cliffs was already boarded up in 1943.**
US Army photographs

THE BUNGALOW ON THE CLIFF, WORBARROW

Above left: **From the south, 1943.**

Above right: **From the north-east. This was the last building along the Worbarrow cliffs, above Sheepleaze. 1943.**

US Army photographs

RANGE OF COTTAGES, BESIDE TRACK INTO WORBARROW, 180 YARDS FROM THE BEACH

Below: **From the south-east, with Flower's Barrow hill-fort on the skyline behind Sheepleaze (left) and the Bungalow (centre) in the middle distance. Note there was a lozenge-shaped date stone to the left of the drain-pipe. One of the cottages was the home of Reggie Ware, a soldier of the Great War. 1943.** US Army photograph

Right: **The same view in 1970, with the Bungalow barely visible as a scatter of bricks, but plus a Mark Two Centurion tank of the late 1940s.** Photograph: Rodney Legg

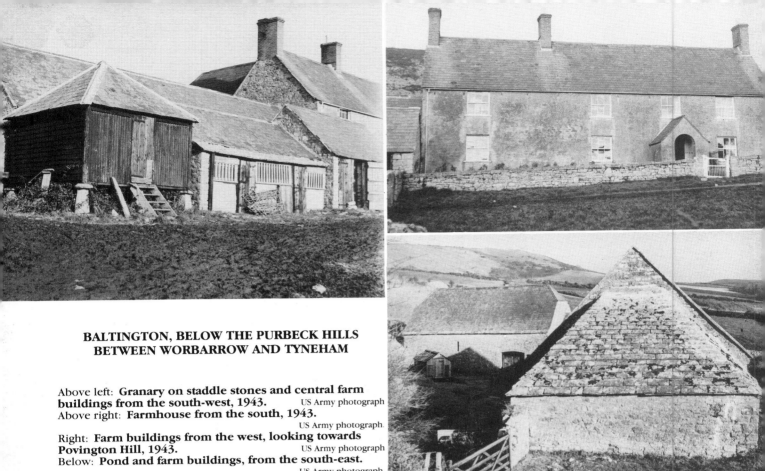

BALTINGTON, BELOW THE PURBECK HILLS
BETWEEN WORBARROW AND TYNEHAM

Above left: **Granary on staddle stones and central farm buildings from the south-west, 1943.** US Army photograph

Above right: **Farmhouse from the south, 1943.** US Army photograph.

Right: **Farm buildings from the west, looking towards Povington Hill, 1943.** US Army photograph

Below: **Pond and farm buildings, from the south-east.** US Army photograph

Opposite bottom: **The same view in 1972, though back from the dried-out pond.** Photograph: Rodney Legg

Opposite top: **General view from the west, 1972.** Photograph: Rodney Legg

'UP UNDER BARROW', BETWEEN WORBARROW AND BALTINGTON

Above left: **From the north, 1943.** US Army photograph

Above right: **From the south, 1943. Its delightful local name, which perfectly describes the idyllic location, was frowned upon by the Ordnance Survey and never made it on to the map.** US Army photograph

SOUTH EGLISTON, BETWEEN TYNEHAM AND KIMMERIDGE

Below: **From the south-west, 1968.** Photograph: Monica Hutchings

WORBARROW BAY
AND (SITE OF) SEA COTTAGES

Right: **Demolition of the ruin of the Miller family's Sea Cottage at Worbarrow was almost total, leaving only a grassy platform with not even a full rectangle of foundations. Much less remains of the two boat-houses, one the fishermen's and the other the estate's, which formerly stood in the foreground and can be glimpsed in some of the earlier photographs. Beyond, however, the view to Flower's Barrow ramparts still performs, with its cliffs of coloured sand. From the south-east. 1992.**
Photograph: Rodney Legg

END OF THE ROAD
AT WORBARROW BAY

Below: **Parked on a knoll a hundred yards north-west of the site of the Victorian Coast Guard Station is a vehicle of HM Coastguard. The stone display-plinth is for the benefit of visitors and shows the sites of the buildings of the seaboard hamlet, where almost all visible history has been wiped from the ground. The view is from the east, across Worbarrow Bay to Mupe Rocks (far left), Cockpit Head (behind plinth), Arish Mell Gap (to the right of it), and the chalk cliffs rising to Flower's Barrow (far right). 1992**
Photograph: Rodney Legg

WORBARROW TOUT AND PONDFIELD COVE

Above: The conical Worbarrow Tout outcrop, here carrying a number '3' target, projects seawards and shelters Worbarrow Bay from the south-easterlies. Pondfield Cove, however, faces that way (near left) and often has completely different wave patterns. The top of the beach is still physically cut-off, for vehicular purposes at any rate, by a double set of concrete dragon's teeth anti-tank obstacles dating from the invasion defences of 1940. Seen from the north-east, from the lower slopes of Gold Down. 1992.

SHEEP ON THE SUMMIT OF GAD CLIFF

Left: The inclined strata of Gad Cliff form a mile-long line of jagged crags, this being the summit at 435 feet. Beyond at sea level, with the white water, are the ledges of Long Ebb with Broad Bench behind. Next, and last in the mist, is Kimmeridge Bay. From the west. 1992.

WAGON ROCK

Below: Midway along the shore beneath Gad Cliff, about one thousand yards east of Pondfield Cove, is a slight promontory with a particularly chunky piece of foreshore. This is Wagon Rock (centre, in the splash-zone). The undercliff here is of considerable width, more than a hundred yards, and varies between the active scree slopes from the crags crumbling from above (bottom left) to grassy ribs of consolidated ground (bottom right). Seen from the clifftop to the north. 1992.

Photographs: Rodney Legg

The Tyneham Coast

PONDFIELD COVE AND GOLD DOWN
Above: **Pondfield Cove and Gold Down at the west end of Gad Cliff, from Worbarrow Tout – with Hobarrow, Kimmeridge Bay and Swyre Head in the distance. About 1960.**
Photograph: Frederick G. Masters

TYNEHAM CAP AND BRANDY BAY
Above: **The 550 feet summit of Tyneham Cap (on the skyline, left of centre) with Brandy Bay below, seen from Gad Cliff. 1972.**
Photograph: Rodney Legg

GATE HANGING FROM GAD CLIFF
Right: **Metal gate 400 feet above the sea at the top of Gad Cliff, above the limestone crags. Beyond is the Purbeck coast – Brandy Bay, Hobarrow Bay, Kimmeridge Bay and St Alban's Head. 1972.**
Photograph: Rodney Legg

THE CRAGS OF GAD

Gad Cliff from the south-east, showing the grey shale cliffs at Hobarrow in the foreground with Brandy Bay beyond, dominated by the yellow limestone crags that form the 400 feet summit of Gad Cliff. From this direction its shape fits its name perfectly, a 'gad' being a quarryman's wedge.1983.

Photograph: Colin Graham

Left: A smoother top-line to Gad Cliff, from the foothills of Tyneham Cap with Brandy Bay beneath. Wagon Rock is the promontory jutting seawards on the other side of the bay. Worbarrow Tout pokes out from behind with Mupe Rocks projecting beyond. Seen from the east. Peregrine falcons continued to nest on these crags during the 1970s years when the populations crashed due to dieldrin and other agrochemicals – saved by the Royal Armoured Corps tank gunnery ranges holding the agricultural revolution at bay. 1966.

Photograph: Monica Hutchings

TYNEHAM CAP and GAD CLIFF

Gad Cliff rearing into the sky, in an otherwise rather
pedestrian view of the outcrops, seen from the east at
Tyneham Cap. The summit is about 430 feet high. Note
the tilt of the inclined strata, which has created the most
dramatic mile of clifftop in the Isle of Purbeck. The
coastal footpath edges towards it, through the long grass.
Far left is the western side of Brandy Bay with Wagon
Rock at sea level, on the promontory. Beyond Worbarrow
Bay (left to right) are Mupe Rocks, Cockpit Head at the
eastern end of Bindon Hill, Arish Mell Gap, and the
western side of Flower's Barrow. 1978.

Photograph: Rodney Legg

FROM TYNEHAM CAP, LOOKING EASTWARDS

Above: **The view from its coastal slope, across the south-eastern extremity of Tyneham parish, which includes the headlands and ledges at Long Ebb (right, on the far side of the first bit of sea which is the inner part of Brandy Bay) and then Broad Bench (beyond the next inlet, which is Hobarrow Bay). All this area, including the undercliff and the upper sweep of the hills, is in the parish of Tyneham. Beyond is the coast of the rest of south-west Purbeck, including Kimmeridge Bay (centre) with the Clavell Tower and behind it the shale cliffs to St Alban's Head. 1978.**
Photograph: Rodney Legg

RAF RADAR STATION, ABOVE SOUTH EGLISTON

Opposite, above: **Concrete footings and debris of the Royal Air Force Radar Station built at the top of the ridge above Egliston Gwyle in 1941. It is on the 450 feet contour at Ordnance Survey map reference SY 900 801. This was established as an additional facility to correlate sightings and angles with the primary radars on the promontories at St Alban's Head and Portland Bill. It was particularly useful in directing the gun-laying and interception of German E-boat incursions aimed at Allied shipping sheltering in Weymouth Bay. Seen from the north-east with Tyneham Cap in the background, half a mile to the west. 1992.**

Opposite: **The view from the RAF Radar Station above South Egliston. It is not particularly inspiring as Dorset scenery goes, but covers the entire eastern approaches to Weymouth Bay and Portland Harbour. The slight projection into the English Channel (just right of centre) is Broad Bench, with the woodland of Egliston Gwyle in front of it in the middle distance. From due south. 1992.**
Photographs: Rodney Legg

ANCIENT HILLTOP CROSS-ROADS

Above: At 382 feet on the ridge nearly a mile east of Tyneham Cap, this is at the eastern extremity of the Army ranges in the parish of Steeple (map reference SY 905 802). This is the track that led inland to Lutton. Another dropped to the south-west to South Egliston. A third went north-east to Steeple Leaze and Steeple village. The fourth went east to the road junction on the top of the hill above Kimmeridge. Seen from the south. 1992.

PURBECK STONE GATE-POST

Left: In the remains of an old stone wall, this typical Purbeck gate had slits for wooden fence-bars. It lies towards the seaward end of the wall that runs upwards from the woods immediately south of Tyneham House, to the west of Tyneham Cap (map reference SY 889 798). From the south. 1992.

RUINS OF SUMMER-HOUSE

Left, bottom: One-time barn and formerly a summer-house for the Bond family of Tyneham House, this little building stood on the western foothills of Tyneham Cap, immediately south-east of the stone pictured above. There was a rounded corner, facing the main view which is south-west over the Gad undercliff and Brandy Bay. The little window (opposite corner) faced Tyneham Cap and was blocked when the building became a barn. Seen from the south-west. 1992.

CHARNEL PILLBOX

Opposite: 1940 anti-invasion machine-gun post on the western cliff at Charnel, in the south-east corner of Tyneham parish (map reference SY 899 789). The seawards view, from the west, is of Kimmeridge Bay and the Clavell Tower, and the view looking inland – to Tyneham Cap – is from the south-east. 1992.

Photographs: Rodney Legg

THE RANGE BOUNDARY

Above: **Security fencing and razor wire at the gate, in Kimmeridge parish, at the south-eastern extremity of the Lulworth and East Holme tank gunnery ranges (map reference SY 904 792). Next on the civilian side of the fence is the British Petroleum oil-well that has been in production since 1959, tapping an underground reservoir 1,790 feet down in the Cornbrash limestone. Stepping through the gate is Peter Shaw, former publisher of Punch, in the week when that national institution suspended publication. Seen from the east, from the end of Kimmeridge public footpath number 17. 1992.**

Photograph: Rodney Legg

KIMMERIDGE LIFEBOAT STATION

Right: **Cliffside spring tapped by the Kimmeridge lifeboat crew for their water supply. Only a platform remains on the ground to the north-west to show the site of their boat-house, though still with an iron railing. The late-Victorian Kimmeridge Lifeboat Station was on the western side of Kimmeridge Bay and actually inside the parish of Tyneham in a hollow on the northern cliffs of Charnel (map reference SY 901 791). The culvert, with running water, is seen from the south. 1992.**

Photograph: Rodney Legg

HOBARROW BAY AND LONG EBB

Left: **The shale-shelf that is the shore of Hobarrow Bay with the little headland of Long Ebb projecting at the end of the beach. This is Tyneham's south-east coast. Next is Brandy Bay and beyond it the mile-long Gad Cliff extending as a wall of stone to the promontory at Worbarrow Tout. Mupe Bay and Cockpit Head are beyond, with Worbarrow Bay hidden from view. Seen from the east, from beside the coast path at map reference SY 897 790. 1992.**

Photograph: Rodney Legg

TYNEHAM CAP

Right: **Though on the coast, Tyneham Cap has not quite been reached by it, and appears in profile as an immense mound of green. Half a mile of long, windswept grass marks the western approach and ascent. Seen from the west, from the coast path that runs just inside the landward lip of Gad Cliff, from map reference SY 887 797. 1992.**

Photograph: Rodney Legg

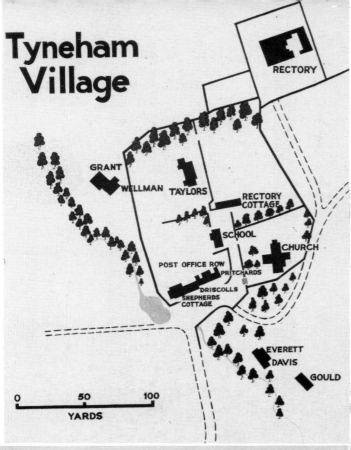

Tyneham Village

Tyneham

MAP OF TYNEHAM VILLAGE

Left: **Showing the village centre clustered around the church. North is on the right. Tyneham Farm was 250 yards south of the Post Office, beside the left-hand track, and Tyneham House 750 yards east-south-east, below the scale-line. The map is nailed to the Post Office gate, 1983.**

Photograph: Colin Graham

SCHOOL TREAT FROM CREECH GRANGE

Below left: **School treat to Tyneham, and presumably the seaside at Worbarrow Bay, from the other Bond family estate on the north side of the Purbeck Hills at Creech Grange. About 1900.** Photograph: Dorset County Museum

SKULL FOUND AT MOUNT MEAD

Below right: **Former Tyneham resident – it is the only parish in Dorset which now records a nil population on the electoral roll. This skull was found at Mount Mead, about 1900.** Photograph: Dorset County Museum

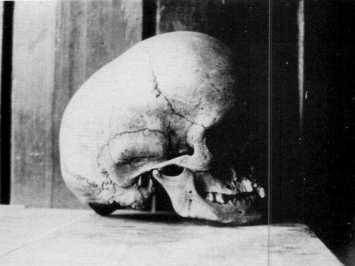

POST OFFICE ROW, TYNEHAM

Opposite page: **From the south-east, about 1900.**
Photograph: Dorset County Museum

Above: **The same view, about 1938. Note the concrete telephone box by the second gate.**
Photograph: Rodney Legg collection

Below: **And the same view in 1943.**   US Army photograph

Left: **South-west corner, the Shepherd's Cottage, in 1970.**
Photograph: Colin Graham

POST OFFICE ROW, TYNEHAM

Left: **The south end of the row, Shepherd's Cottage, from the south-east, 1969.** Photograph: Rodney Legg

Above: **The centre and south end of the row, showing the rear from the west, 1943.** US Army photograph

Below: **The frontage of the centre and north end of the row, Driscolls' and Pritchards', from the east, 1970.** Photograph: Rodney Legg

Opposite top: **The row from the south-east before 'renovation', about 1980. 'Please credit', the photograph says, HQ Royal Armoured Corps Centre – for it or the mess?**

Opposite bottom: **The same view after 'renovation' had become 'reduction', removing the gable ends. Photographed in 1983.** Photograph: Colin Graham

TELEPHONE BOX AND POLE, TYNEHAM

Above left: **The concrete box outside Post Office row, with a notice 'Danger Keep Out : There are bombs and unexploded shells inside. They can kill you.' The rector swore at engineer Wilson Coombes who erected the box in 1928. Pictured in 1967.**

Photograph: Rodney Legg

Above right: **Tyneham's first telephone pole, beside the Post Office parking space, in the 1930s. By 1943 its top supported 16 caps. The oak between the churchyard steps and the village water tap was planted in 1911 by Margaret Bond to replace an old and dangerous elm tree which her father had felled.**

Photograph: Rodney Legg collection

Left: **The box after renovation, though with a modern typeface replacing the original serifs, from the north-west, 1983.**

Photograph: Colin Graham

THE COKE-HUT,
TYNEHAM CHURCHYARD
Opposite page

Right: **18th century watchkeeper's window and hut in the north-west corner of Tyneham churchyard, seen from the south-east, 1971. This rare countryside treasure has since disappeared without reason or record, leaving only a concrete floor. It was on the property of the Church Commissioners, rather than that of the Ministry of Defence, though at the time of writing the author has no information on which of them to curse.**

Photograph: Rodney Legg

EVERETT AND DAVIS COTTAGES, TYNEHAM

Above: **From the south-west, 1943.**

US Army photograph

Below: **From the north-west, 1983.**

Photograph: Colin Graham

GOULD'S COTTAGE, TYNEHAM

Above: **From the south, 1943.**

US Army photograph

Below: **From the north-west, 1983.**
Photograph: Colin Graham (This ruin, incidentally, is omitted in error from the 1963 6-inch Ordnance Survey map.)

THE CHURCH, TYNEHAM

All on the double page spread overleaf

First page top: **Sketch of the church before the addition by Rev. William Bond of the south transept in the 1840s, from the south-west.**
First page, bottom left: **The chancel and altar, 1943.**

US Army photograph.

First page, bottom right: **The organ (since moved to Steeple church).**

US Army photograph.

Second page, top: **From the north-west, showing a degree of neglect with ivy climbing the walls and longish grass, 1943.**

US Army photograph

Second page, centre: **The same view in 1983.**
Second page, bottom left: **From the south-west, 1983.**
Second page, bottom right: **Feudal state memorial to Mrs Bond's faithful servant, Elizabeth Tarrant, who died in 1769.**

1983 photographs: Colin Graham

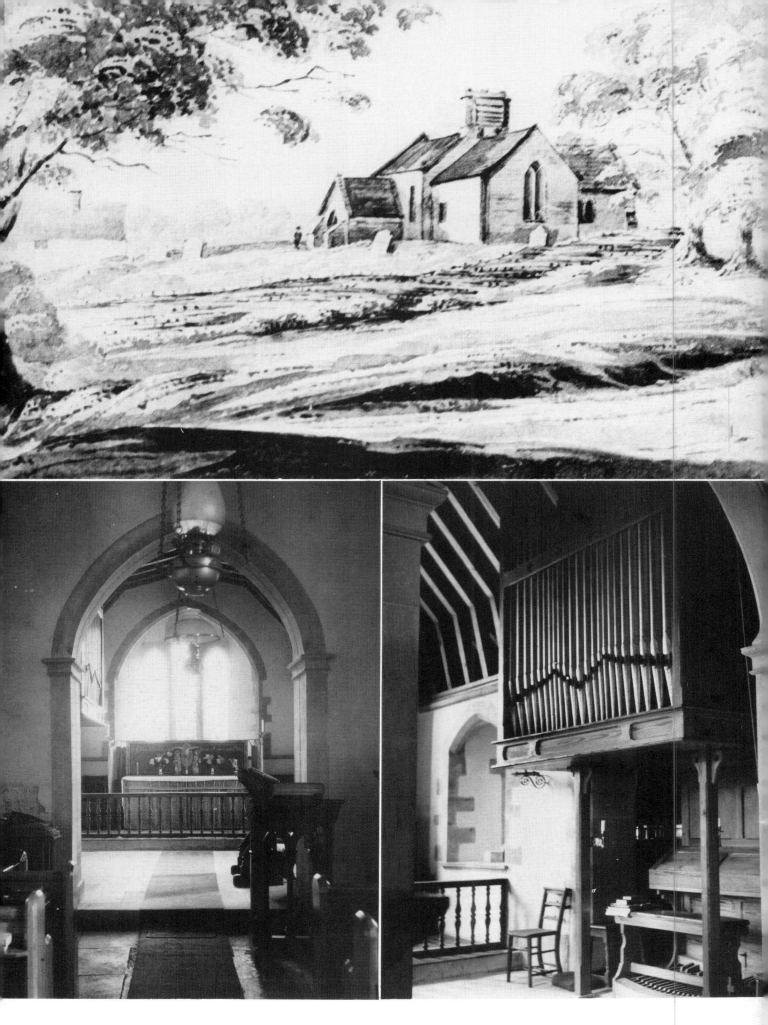

Near this Place Lye y̓ Body of
ELIZABETH TARRANT
Servant to M.rs BOND of
Tineham in which Station
She continued 34 Years.

To y̓ Memory of her Prudence
Honesty, & Industry,
this Monument is erected
She died August y̓ 2.d 1769
in y̓ 54 Year of her Age

TYNEHAM'S PARISH CHURCH OF SAINT MARY

Right and extending into next page:
Line of early Victorian Caen stone memorials to eminent Bonds. They start with William Bond, metropolitan police magistrate and recorder of Poole and Wareham, **followed by Rev Henry Bond, vicar of South Petherton, and barrister Thomas Bond. Last and with stongest claim to be here is Rev William Bond, 1757-1852, and rector of this parish for the last 57 of those years. 1992 photograph.**

Below: **Commemorative inscription on the Bible which closed for use in this church on the second Sunday before Christmas in 1943. 1992 photograph.**

Foot of page: **Churchyard memorial to last private owner of Tyneham, Ralph Bond, 1880-1952, and wife Evelyn who died two years later. 1992 photograph.**

Bottom right: **Stained glass to Algy, Ralph's brother Algernon Bond who was a year older and was with him at Eton. A fine horseman, Algy would be seriously wounded at the siege of Ladysmith in the Boer War, and in thanksgiving for his survival his parents installed the pipe-organ which has now been moved to Steeple church. 1992.**

Photographs: Rodney Legg

This Holy Bible, the last to be used in the Church of St. Mary, was restored by the Royal Armoured Corps Gunnery School in 1981 in memory of the Parishioners of Tyneham and Worbarrow, through the generosity of the Public and the Bond Family

The Parishioners

H M G. Bond
E M C. Bond
Mr and Mrs Ralph Bond
Mr and Mrs William Bond
Miss Margaret Bond
The Misses Blake
Mr and Mrs Churchill
Mr and Mrs Curtis
Joe Dands
George and Ellen Davis
Mr and Mrs Phillip Draper
Gwendoline Driscoll
Maud Ellis
George Lily and Arthur Everett
The Rev and Mrs Flend
Tom, Virtue and John Gould
Henry, Marjorie, Arthur Grant
Cyril Griffiths
James and Edith Herd
Charlotte and Helena Hole
William Holland
Herbert and Jessie House
Gerald, Gwen and Poppy House
William House
Arthur and Rose House
Sylvia House
Mr and Mrs Howard

Percy Howard
George Howard
Percy and Ellen Kerley
Robert and Reginald Longman
Charles Meech
Jack and Alice Miller
Charles and Harriet Miller
Thomas and Minnie Miller
Winifred and Beatrice Minterne
Tom Minterne
The Rev and Mrs Money
Mr and Mrs Burrant
Mr and Mrs Pritchard and son Arthur
Mrs Regner
Walter and Kate Smith
Arthur and Phillis Stockley
Mr and Mrs James Tassell
William Elizabeth and Helen Taylor
Mr and Mrs Albert Toms
Mr and Mrs Upshall
Reginald Ware
Mrs Wheeler
Bob and Alice Wellman
Ernest and Evelyn Whitlock
William Frend

✠
SACRED TO THE MEMORY OF
WILLIAM RALPH GARNEYS BOND, OF TYNEHAM
BORN 12TH DEC. 1880 — DIED 10TH FEB. 1952
AND OF EVELYN ISABEL HIS WIFE
BORN 11TH SEPT 1884 — DIED 3RD SEPT 1954

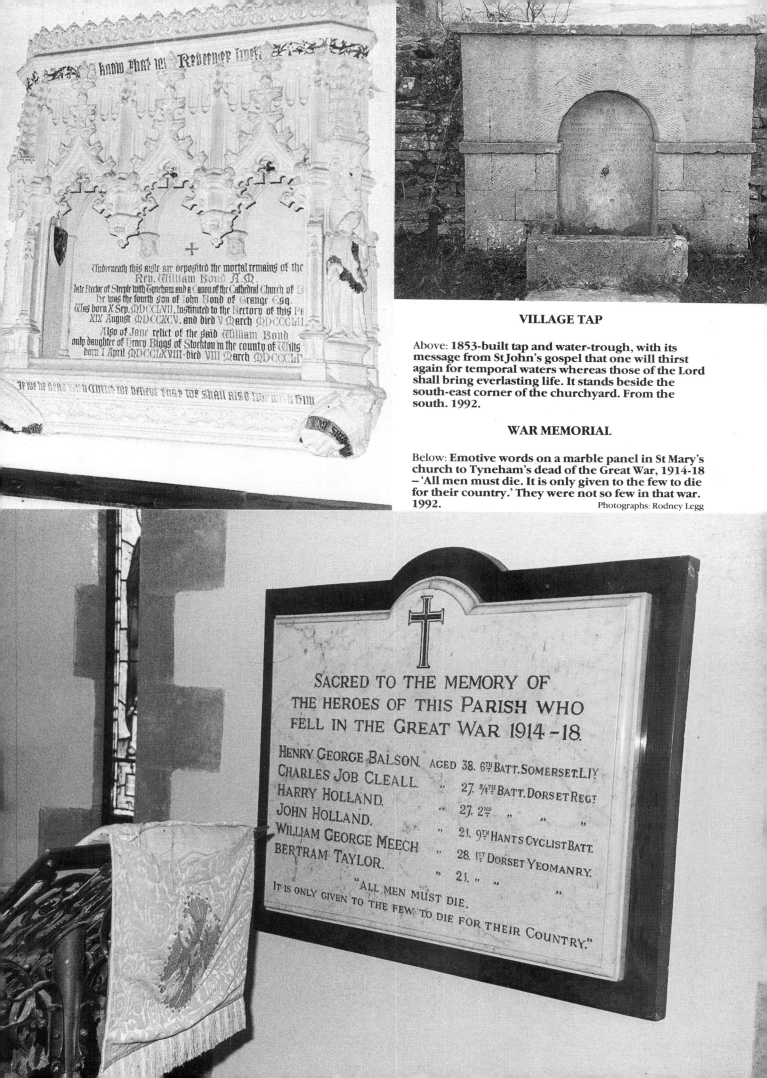

VILLAGE TAP

Above: **1853-built tap and water-trough, with its message from St John's gospel that one will thirst again for temporal waters whereas those of the Lord shall bring everlasting life. It stands beside the south-east corner of the churchyard. From the south. 1992.**

WAR MEMORIAL

Below: **Emotive words on a marble panel in St Mary's church to Tyneham's dead of the Great War, 1914-18 – 'All men must die. It is only given to the few to die for their country.' They were not so few in that war. 1992.**

Photographs: Rodney Legg

SACRED TO THE MEMORY OF
THE HEROES OF THIS PARISH WHO
FELL IN THE GREAT WAR 1914 –18.

HENRY GEORGE BALSON.   AGED 38.   6TH BATT. SOMERSET. L.I.Y
CHARLES JOB CLEALL.   "   27.   2/4TH BATT. DORSET REGT
HARRY HOLLAND.   "   27.   2ND   "   "   "
JOHN HOLLAND.   "   21.   9TH HANTS CYCLIST BATT.
WILLIAM GEORGE MEECH   "   28.   1ST DORSET YEOMANRY.
BERTRAM TAYLOR.   "   21.   "   "   "

"ALL MEN MUST DIE,
IT IS ONLY GIVEN TO THE FEW TO DIE FOR THEIR COUNTRY."

TYNEHAM BACK PORCHES

Above: **Behind the cottages of Post Office Row. From the south. 1992.**
Photograph: Rodney Legg

TYNEHAM CORBEL-STONE

Above: **In Rectory Cottages, above a downstairs fireplace, between it and a door. The corbel-stone (left, centre) has come from a more formal piece of architecture, probably rebuilding at the nearby church, as has the squared ashlar next to it (immediately to the right). From the south. 1992.**
Photograph: Rodney Legg

TYNEHAM FIREPLACES

Below: **In Post Office Row, where a benefit of dereliction is that upstairs and downstairs are visible at the same time. The bedroom has a cast-iron Victorian hearth, but in the living room the modern inset brickwork of circa 1940 would have been someone's pride and joy. From the south. 1992.**
Photograph: Rodney Legg

TYNEHAM MEDIAEVAL PISCINA

Above: **Primitive and early, from the thirteenth century, this is one of the few objects from the original parish church, still in situ in the wall, on the east side of the north transept of St Mary's. From the west. 1992.**
Photograph: Rodney Legg

THE SCHOOL, TYNEHAM

Above left: **From the north-west, 1943.**   US Army photograph

Above right: **From the west, 1983, when it was in use as a small museum, though with displays that put a gloss on Tyneham's tragedy.**
Photograph: Colin Graham

RECTORY COTTAGES, TYNEHAM

Right: **From the rear, the north west, in 1943.**
US Army photograph

Near right: **From the same position, 1983 – hardly even a picturesque ruin.**   Photograph: Colin Graham

Below: **Formerly attractive frontage, from the east, 1943.**
US Army photograph. (This ruin, incidentally, is omitted in error from the 1963 edition of the 6-inch Ordnance Survey map.)

THE RECTORY, TYNEHAM

Above: **From the east, 1943.** US Army photograph

Left: **From the same position, 1972. It had been burnt down in the 1960s, by vandals rather than the army, as the author was reminded by a heckler at a public meeting. 'It wouldn't have happened if the Rector had still been living there,'** he replied.

Photograph: Rodney Legg

Overleaf, top: **From the south-east, 1943.**

US Army photograph.

Overleaf, centre left: **Northern outbuildings, from the east. 1943.** US Army photograph

Overleaf, bottom left: **Same outbuildings, from inside the cobbled courtyard. 1943.** US Army photograph

THE RECTORY, TYNEHAM

(See page 61 for three captions)

Below: **The rector's garage. 1943.** US Army photograph

TAYLOR'S COTTAGES
TYNEHAM

Above: **From the south, 1943.** US Army photograph

Below: **From almost the same position in 1983.**
Photograph: Colin Graham

Right: **From the east, 1943.** US Army photograph

GRANT AND WELLMAN COTTAGES, TYNEHAM

Above left: **From the south, 1943.**   US Army photograph

Above right: **From the north 1943.**   US Army photograph

Left: **From the east, 1983.**   Photograph: Colin Graham

CART SHED, WEST OF TYNEHAM FARM

Below: **Shed to the west of Tyneham Farm, on the south side of the Gwyle bridge beside the track to Worbarrow. Seen from the south-east, 1943. The boy appears to be Geoffrey Churchill, the farmer's younger son.**
US Army photograph

BRIDGE OVER THE GWYLE STREAM, TYNEHAM

Above: **The east side of the bridge, to the west of Tyneham Farm, in 1971.**
Photograph: Rodney Legg

TYNEHAM FARM

Above: **From the south-west, 1943.** US Army photograph

Left: **From the same position in 1971.** Photograph: Rodney Legg

Below: **Central barn at Tyneham Farm, from the eastern farmyard, 1943.** US Army photograph

EASTERN FARMYARD, TYNEHAM FARM

Above: **From the south, 1943, with the Purbeck Hills behind.**
US Army photograph

Left: **From the south-east, 1971, showing remarkably little change for a building at Tyneham.** Photograph: Rodney Legg

Below: **Distant view from the south, 1971, with the rusting hulk of a Churchill tank in the foreground.**
Photograph: Rodney Legg

SOUTH RANGE OF BUILDINGS, TYNEHAM FARM

Top: **South range of farm buildings, from the north, 1943.**
US Army photograph

Above: **The left end of the buildings in the top picture, 1972, with the weeds appearing almost to have reached the roof.**
Photograph: Colin Graham

COW-STALLS, TYNEHAM FARM
Below: **Stone-roofed cow-stalls, from the south, 1943.**
US Army photograph

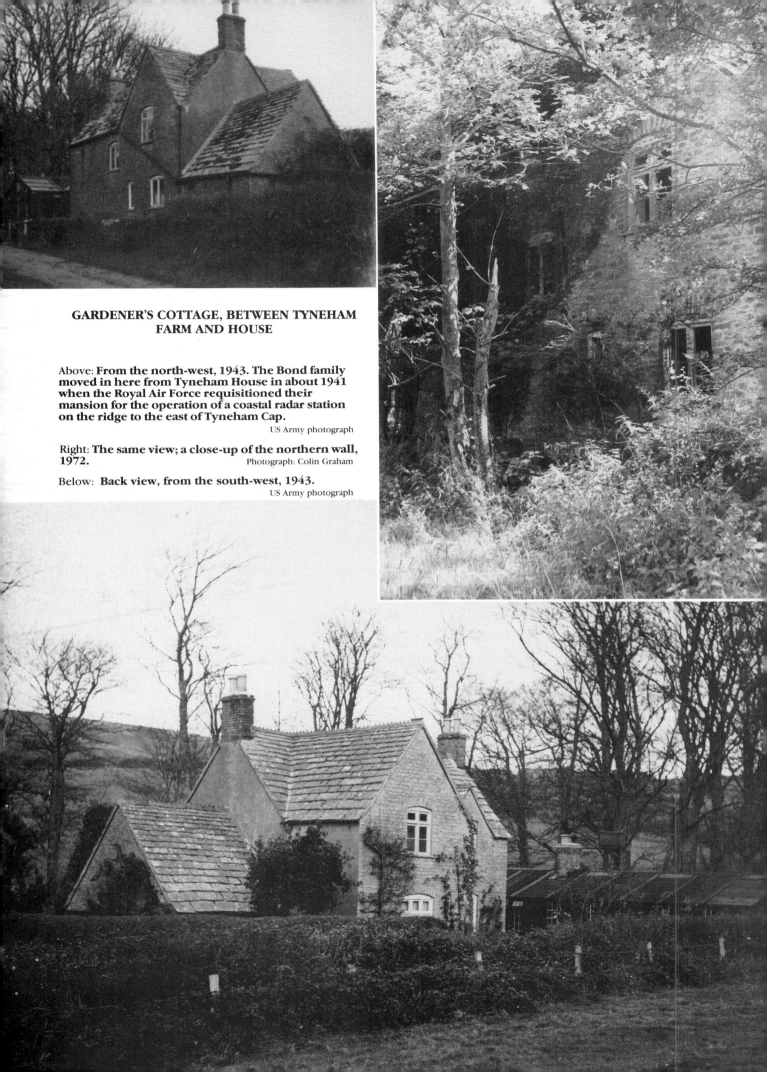

GARDENER'S COTTAGE, BETWEEN TYNEHAM FARM AND HOUSE

Above: **From the north-west, 1943. The Bond family moved in here from Tyneham House in about 1941 when the Royal Air Force requisitioned their mansion for the operation of a coastal radar station on the ridge to the east of Tyneham Cap.**

US Army photograph

Right: **The same view; a close-up of the northern wall, 1972.** Photograph: Colin Graham

Below: **Back view, from the south-west, 1943.**

US Army photograph

TIMBER HALL BESIDE GARDENER'S COTTAGE

Above: **From the east, with Gardener's Cottage behind, 1943.**
US Army photograph

Right: **From the same position in 1972, with only the gate-posts and chimney of the hut, though the sycamore trees and cottage were still standing.**
Photograph: Colin Graham

TYNEHAM HOUSE GROUNDS

Right: **Outbuilding near Gardener's Cottage, from the north, 1972.**
Photograph: Colin Graham

Right below: **Same building, from the south-west. 1972.**
Photograph: Colin Graham

Below: **Gothic gate-post in the sycamores. 1972.**
Photograph: Colin Graham

TYNEHAM HOUSE

Above: **From the north-east, after fashionable high windows had been installed along the ground floor of the Elizabethan frontage. Taking a stroll is Thomas Bond, brother of the owner, Prebendary John Bond. He is standing beside the 1583-built east porch, but look at the gleaming new stonework of the north porch (right). This embellishment can only be a few months old, if that, and means that the shot is an exceedingly early landscape photograph, dating from 1861-62.** Photograph: Dorset County Museum

Below: **Mullioned-window outbuilding, from the south-east, 1943.** US Army photograph

Below: **The 1861 porch (centre) and north wing, from the north, 1943.** US Army photograph

TYNEHAM HOUSE

Right: **From the north-east, in balmy days with the summertime appearance of potted palms. The house was acclaimed as one of the most beautiful country houses in Dorset. Tyneham Great Wood is glimpsed beyond. August 1912.**
Photograph: C.J. Cornish Brown

Below: **From the south-east, in a wider view of strategically-placed palms and not a leaf out of place. The Elizabethan frontage and porch, built by Henry Williams in 1583, are seen from the edge of Tyneham Great Wood, August 1912.**
Photograph: C.S. Cornish Brown

TYNEHAM HOUSE
Ground Floor Plan

Uses and names as in
the early 1900s

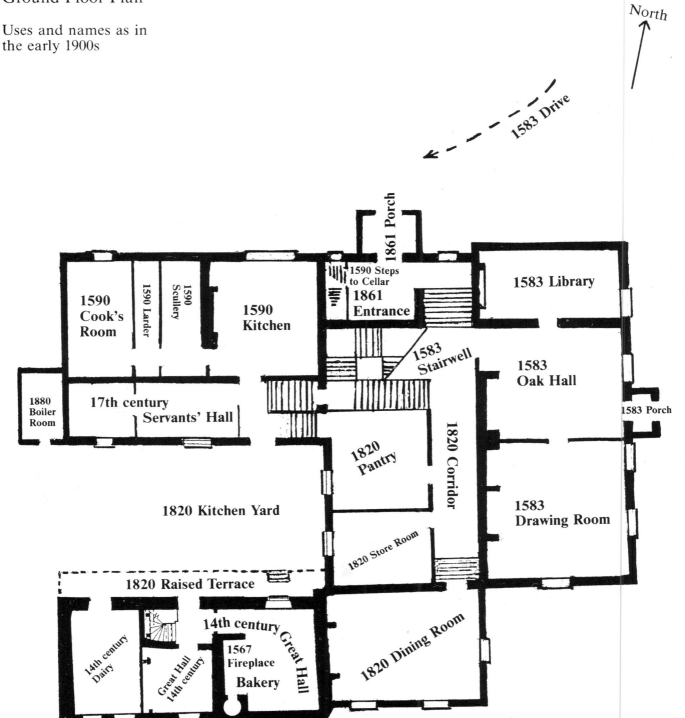

North

1583 Drive

1861 Porch

1590 Steps to Cellar

1861 Entrance

1590 Cook's Room

1590 Larder

1590 Scullery

1590 Kitchen

1583 Stairwell

1583 Library

1880 Boiler Room

17th century Servants' Hall

1583 Oak Hall

1583 Porch

1820 Lawn

1820 Pantry

1820 Corridor

1583 Drawing Room

1820 Kitchen Yard

1820 Store Room

1820 Raised Terrace

14th century Dairy

Great Hall 14th century

1567 Fireplace Bakery

14th century Great Hall

1820 Dining Room

TYNEHAM HOUSE

Above and opposite: **Plans of the ground and first floor
rooms of Tyneham House, showing the development of
the building and the names of the rooms. Some of the last
Bond family users are identified. William Henry Bond
inherited Tyneham House and the valley estate in 1898.
Compiled from books and photographs with the
assistance of Lilian M.G. Bond and Rowena Preston.**

Graphics: Rodney Legg

TYNEHAM HOUSE
First Floor Plan

Uses and names as in
the early 1900s

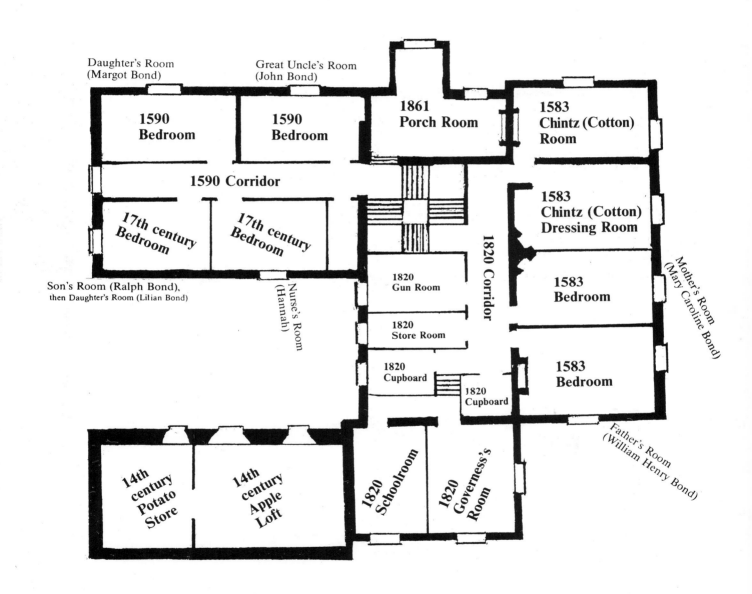

Daughter's Room
(Margot Bond)

Great Uncle's Room
(John Bond)

1590
Bedroom

1590
Bedroom

1861
Porch Room

1583
**Chintz (Cotton)
Room**

1590 Corridor

1583
**Chintz (Cotton)
Dressing Room**

**17th century
Bedroom**

**17th century
Bedroom**

Son's Room (Ralph Bond),
then Daughter's Room (Lilian Bond)

Nurse's Room
(Hannah)

1820
Gun Room

1820 Corridor

1583
Bedroom

Mother's Room
(Mary Caroline Bond)

1820
Store Room

1820
Cupboard

1820
Cupboard

1583
Bedroom

**14th
century
Potato
Store**

**14th
century
Apple
Loft**

1820
Schoolroom

1820
Governess's
Room

Father's Room
(William Henry Bond)

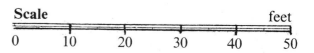

Scale
feet

0   10   20   30   40   50

57

TYNEHAM HOUSE

Above: **From the east, showing the full Elizabethan frontage at its most immaculate, though with the addition of the 1820 dining room block (far left),then Victorian windows, and now well into the era of the lawn-mower. For a complete contrast, look opposite. August 1912.**
Photograph: C.J. Cornish Brown

1 Queen's Avenue – Dorchester

I think you may both like to have this very inadequate memoir. So send it with my best wishes –
Lilian M.G. Bond

Left: **In her own hand – letter to Monica Hutchings from Miss Lilian M.G. Bond, late of Tyneham House and author of a booklet on her brother, William Ralph Garneys Bond [1880-1952], and a nostalgic chronicle of life in the vanished community of 'Tyneham' which was an evocative celebration of its lost 'permanence and peace'.**
Source: Rodney Legg collection

TYNEHAM HOUSE

Right: **From the north-west, showing the 1861-built porch (centre) and the north gable-end of the Elizabethan wing of Tyneham House at the end of its post-war neglect and dereliction. Demolition was about to follow but the photograph is evidence that the house was still largely intact and certainly repairable. Boarded-up and with a few stone tiles missing, it is otherwise much the same as in its 1943 picture on the opposite page. In a few months, however, it would be reduced to ruins as is shown on the far photograph on the next page. Perpetration of this outrage was achieved largely through dubious connivance of the Ministry of Works and the Ministry of Defence – as the War Department had become – aided by the reason that it was out of sight and out of mind. As Monica Hutchings wrote:**

'Very few people indeed knew of the exact whereabouts of Tyneham House, and fewer had ever seen it. Hidden in tall trees by Tyneham Great Wood, in a fold in the hills behind Army Gate No. 18 and a good half mile from the remains of the village, it had not been in the public eye like the church, which had been kept weather proofed and in repair in spite of the fact that it was closer to the actual firing.' 1967. Photograph: Monica Hutchings

Above: **Elizabethan east front after demolition, 1972.**

Photograph: Colin Graham

Below left: **The north wing and outbuildings, from the north-west, 1943.**

US Army photograph

Below right: **The north porch and centre of house from the same angle, 1972.**

Photograph: Rodney Legg

Above: **From the south, with the hawthorn in bloom, 7 June 1924. Note the heavy growth of creepers up the walls.**

Photograph: E. Dodshon

Right: **Palms above the pond and the south-east corner of the house, 1943.**

US Army photograph

Below left: **First floor room at north end of Elizabethan east wing, showing panelling and fireplace in west wall.**

Ministry of Works photograph

Below right: **Same room, north wall (the pictures join in the middle) with shuttered window and 'Smoking Strictly Prohibited' notice.**

Ministry of Works photograph

MEDIAEVAL WING, TYNEHAM HOUSE

Above: **Rear of Tyneham House, from the west, showing the mediaeval section in the centre-right, 1943.**
US Army photograph

Right: **The centre-right section in 1972, after removal of a stone doorway.**
Photograph: Rodney Legg

Right below: **Detail of the west end of the mediaeval section, from the north, 1972. Note the luxuriant fern growth on the stone roof.**
Photograph: Colin Graham

Below: **Roof timbers, 1951.**
Photograph: Ministry of Works

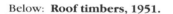

A Media Issue

THE NATIONAL TRUST
FOOTPATH ONLY
TO THE SEA
NO PUBLIC
RIGHT OF WAY
FOR VEHICLES

THE TYNEHAM CAMPAIGN, 1972

Opposite page, top: **Rodney Legg addresses bank holiday crowds in Tyneham car park.**
Photograph: Arthur Grant

Opposite page, nearest: **They also heard Kenneth Allsop, whose last feature article for the Sunday Times, just before he died in May 1973, was about the problems of preserving nature in a peacetime Tyneham.**
Photograph: Colin Graham

Opposite, far side: **The campaigners' dream was Tyneham as a National Trust property, provided that intensive agriculture did not take over from the army.**
Composite photograph: Rodney Legg

Top left: **The slogan said it all, and took Mr Gould far from his native valley.**
Photograph: Colin Graham

Above: **John Gould at Number 10 Downing Street.**
Photograph: Colin Graham

Left: **John Gould approaching Number Ten with a wreath for Harold Wilson, in memory of former Tyneham residents, with Mavis Caver, Philip Watkins, Lord Fenner Brockway and a ragged-looking Rodney Legg. Brian Jackman stands directly behind Lord Brockway.** Photograph: Colin Graham

Povington – Tyneham's heathland hamlet

**COTTAGE BETWEEN REMPSTONE GATE
AND WHITEWAY, POVINGTON**
Above: **From the north, 1943.** US Army photograph

Top right: **From the west, showing an unimproved cob and
thatch dwelling, 1943. There was a well beside the east
wall.** US Army photograph

HOUSE NORTH OF THE TRACK AT WHITEWAY
Right: **The mock-tudor Edwardian dwelling, from the
south, 1943.** US Army photograph

**HOUSE SOUTH OF THE TRACK
AT WHITEWAY, POVINGTON**
Below: **The Victorian stone and slate house from the
north-east, 1943.** US Army photograph

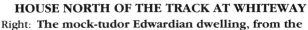

WHITEWAY FARM, POVINGTON
Opposite top: **From the north-east, 1943.** US Army photograph

Opposite near corner: **From the west, dominated by a tall
Scots pine, 1943.** US Army photograph

Opposite far corner: **Farmyard from the north, 1943.**
US Army photograph

COTTAGE BETWEEN THORN BARROW AND POVINGTON FARM

Above: **White-washed brick frontage and heathstone extension, 1943.** US Army photograph

Above right: **Long tiled roof at the rear, the raised coping stones showing that it once had a cladding of thatch. 1943.** US Army photograph

PAIR OF COTTAGES WEST OF POVINGTON FARM

Below: **A brick-rendered cob and thatch building of the early nineteenth century with two stone-roofed porches, the right-hand one being between the two downstairs windows and partly obscured by the young plum trees. The brick cladding extended around the sides but the rear wall was of exposed cob, partly protected by a tiled outhouse and corrugated-iron lean-to.** US Army photograph

FARMSTEAD AT THE HAMLET
WEST OF POVINGTON FARM

Above: **Eighteenth century with substantial stone basis to the left half, with brick upper parts and addition to the right. 1943.**

Right: **The farmyard and barns from the rear.**

US Army photographs

COTTAGE SOUTH OF TRACK
IN THE POVINGTON HAMLET

Below left: **From the north, an exposed cob wall, 1943.**
Below right: **From the south, showing a typical cob and thatch structure, probably eighteenth century, with minor brick cladding and buttressing, plus the cabbage patch. 1943.** US Army photographs

PRIMROSE COTTAGE, POVINGTON

Top left: **Late nineteenth century brick-built cottage on earlier heathstone foundations, with whitewashed frontage and horseshoe over the door. From the south-west, 1943.**

Top right: **From the far side, the north-east, showing the emblem of a primrose flower in the brickwork.**

COTTAGES IN THE PLOT NEXT TO PRIMROSE COTTAGE, POVINGTON

Above: **One of the earliest of the Povington buildings, of seventeenth or early eighteenth century heathstone and thatch, from the south. 1943.**

Right: **From the north-east. 1943.**   US Army photographs

PAIR OF COTTAGES AT POVINGTON

Right: **Early eighteenth century cottages rebuilt in the late nineteenth century; previously thatched. 1943.**

US Army photograph

MEETING ROOM (?) AND COTTAGE, POVINGTON

Below right: **The nineteenth century stone and slate cottage has a one-room extension at the side which had its own path and fenced boundary – though it is too small to have been inhabited and is without its own chimney. It may have been a meeting room.**

US Army photograph

THATCHED COTTAGE AT POVINGTON

Below: **Cob cottage of the early nineteenth century with brick-clad front and back walls, the original mud being exposed at the sides. 1943.**

US Army photograph

COTTAGE, 300 YARDS NORTH NORTH-WEST OF POVINGTON FARM

Below: **Early nineteenth century cottage, of brick and tile construction with a hipped gable. From the south-west. 1943.**

US Army photograph

COTTAGE 400 YARDS NORTH-WEST OF POVINGTON FARM

Below: **Stone first storey with brick second storey that covers the original cob, of eighteenth or early nineteenth century date. Tiled and corrugated iron outbuildings and lean-tos at the rear and east side. 1943.**

US Army photograph

POVINGTON FARM

Above left: **The north wing of the house and north-west outbuilding from the north-west approach. The 'building' glimpsed on the left edge of the page is in fact the dovecote. 1943.** US Army photograph

Above right: **The south wing of the house, from the south – a robust building of the early nineteenth century though a farm had stood on the site for centuries. 1943.** US Army photograph

Right: **The north-west outbuilding and dovecote, seen from the north-east, 1943.** US Army photograph

Below left: **Cart shed, from the north, with duck pool in the foreground, 1943.** US Army photograph

Below right: **Barn adjoining the cart shed (left) from the north-east. 1943.** US Army photograph

Right: **Just about the last cart-load to leave the main barn at the farm, which is seen from the north. A granary stands on staddle-stones to the left, and a long range of corrugated iron cattle stalls stretched off to the right. 1943.** US Army photograph

POVINGTON CLAY PIT

A massive hole has cut through the Tyneham-Steeple parish boundary between Povington Wood and Raymond's Firs (centre background). It operated from 1954 until 1973 without any planning permission, though this was then obtained by English China Clays after pictures of the pit were published in the Dorset County Magazine where it was described as 'the biggest hole in Dorset'. The crane (centre right) is taking ball clay from a seam 80 feet down. Over the years the working moved south-east towards the camera, from the distant left-hand corner which had since been back-filled with waste sand and gravel. The hole is across 110 acres, with a maximum depth of about 150 feet. 1972. Photograph: Colin Graham

Povington Farm was as remote and rustic as any in the parish of Tyneham, and is now in complete ruin, so it makes an appropriate ending to our photographic coverage of these 3,003 acres of forgotten Purbeck.

TYNEHAM is the special South Coast time-warp. Had it not gone under military occupation six days before Christmas in 1943, and then failed to return to peacetime life as had been pledged, I doubt if it would now be hallowed as a place of such sacred memory. Other coastal valleys in western Purbeck, such as at Lulworth and Kimmeridge, have their own charms and nostalgia of the sort that Women's Institutes are so good at gathering.

Tyneham post-1945 could have been much the same; nice, yes, but hardly unique. What brings it the accolade is that it alone has since returned to something approaching the unkempt wilderness of a mediaeval landscape at the fringes of civilisation. The clearance of population from the entire 3,003 acre parish was at the order of Churchill's War Cabinet, for the benefit of the Gunnery Wing of the Royal Armoured Corps Fighting Vehicles School at Lulworth Camp.

They were to train the American and British tank crews who were destined to open the Second Front against the Nazis in Normandy. Co-beneficiaries of the military's good fortune in being allowed to retain their war-gains have been the wildlife, from the roe deer to the birds; everywhere there are birds. Military ecology, paradoxically, can win the green vote. It is well ahead of the county's normal countryside, the land that has since gone through the Agricultural Revolution of ploughing and chemicals, both in the numbers and diversity of its wildlife species.

That is why there are always buzzards circling overhead and why the peregrine falcon came back from near man-inflicted extinction to breed in the Lulworth Ranges ahead of its reappearance in civilian countryside. Other deft swing-wing birds of prey such as the merlin and the hobby never stopped breeding in army lands as their like ceased to be seen in most of lowland England.

Tyneham and the ruins of its scattered farms and cottages have been engulfed in a jungle that is still largely a forbidden land despite the network of permissive weekend and summer holiday paths, called the Lulworth Range

Walks, that are opened when tank firing is suspended. Most of the parish remains far from these paths. Explosions are taken by nature in its stride, as much a part of the way of the world as thunder and lightning, and bird-song beside the trenches is a phenomenon found in the war-poets of Flanders and the Somme.

The other Tyneham paradox is that life there has been remembered with a clarity undiminished by the passing of decades. The minds of those who lived there prior to 1943 remain uncluttered by subsequent events. They are recalled in a soft half-focus that suits the image of a rural idyll. It was a piece of feudal Dorset, still in the fiefdom of the Bond family who had owned its valley for generations, though that was always recounted as a strength rather than anything questionable.

Not that Dorset readily accepted that one of its most cherished coastal valleys would be yielded into perpetual military occupation.

The fall of Tyneham and western Purbeck into military occupation is the most emotive episode of recent Dorset history. The Ministry of Defence lands in south-east Dorset, which form the Royal Armoured Corps Centre, cover a total of 9,601 acres. Of this 7,501 acres comprise the Lulworth and East Holme Ranges; the other 2,100 acres are on the north side of the River Frome at Bovington. The Ministry of Defence holds the freehold of this land, apart from 1,188 acres at Lulworth which are rented.

This depopulated landscape of open downland with miles of heath and sheer cliffs has for years provided Dorset's principal countryside conflict. Several times the case was carried through the corridors of power, with deputations received at the House of Commons and Number Ten Downing Street, and it has resulted in a typical British compromise. This impasse has done nothing to allow home the ageing survivors of wartime evictions, but subsequent generations have been conceded weekend access privileges on a vast scale – with miles of spectacular footpaths and deep-blue, sheltered coves set in the middle of one of Britain's most important military training grounds.

Smugglers and the Coast Guard, 1832

First, however, a potted account of how Tyneham came into the modern world, beginning with its place in the smuggling trade – a cottage industry along this coast.

A brief disturbance on a Lulworth cliff that ended with murder rated only the following short paragraph in a local paper of 1832: "An encounter at Lulworth between a Preventive Officer named Knight and his assistant and a party of smugglers resulted in the officer being thrown over the cliffs. He died soon after being found."

The story was told more fully on a gravestone in Weymouth's Bury Street cemetery. There is no longer any Bury Street cemetery. It was cleared of bones in 1974 and replaced, in the fashion of the decade, by a multi-storey car park. Knight's stone has been rehoused in the town's museum:

Sacred to the Memory of Lieut. Edward Knight, RN, of Folkestone, Kent, Aged 42, who in the execution of his duty as Chief Officer of the Coastguard was wantonly attacked by a body of smugglers near Lulworth on the night of 28th of June, 1832, by whom after being unmercifully beaten he was thrown over the cliff near Durdle Door from the effects of which he died the following day. By his untimely death the public service has lost a valuable and universally respected officer and sincere friend and his wife and family an affectionate husband and kind father.

That memorial comes from the closing years of the smugglers' era. Two centuries of heavy taxation on spirits that brought prosperity to those in a position to evade the excise – the fishermen of the south coast, and those in the manorial homes who financed illicit cargoes, gambling on the fact that four out of five runs came safely through the coastguards' net. The job of landing the kegs and distributing the goods fell to a wider section of the community who played their part in a national network of secret routes and caches. Most of the Purbeck cargoes were shipped out again, across the waters of Poole Harbour, to avoid risk in leaving by the island's easily guarded land exit. Landings were made on the northern harbour shore at Keysworth, West Holton, Lytchett Bay, Hamworthy and Parkstone. The waggon routes inland lay open from these lonely places.

Some loads, however, did go out through the front door of Purbeck. W.M. Hardy recorded in his *Smuggling Days in Purbeck* a rare occurrence of boldness in daylight: "In the year 1796 my grandfather, then a boy ten years old, and living in Wareham, was an eyewitness to a stroke of astonishing bravado and reckless defiance of the law in broad daylight. Well did he remember one day seeing two waggons pass through the main street of the town, coming from the direction of Purbeck and going on to Northport. They were loaded with tubs and the devil-may-care smugglers, with great sticks in their brawny hands, were seated on top of them, evidently ready to defend their property should occasion for doing so arise . . ."

Frequent landings were made on the cliffs and bays of southern Purbeck, especially Worbarrow, Brandy Bay (an apposite name), Kimmeridge, Chapman's Pool, Winspit, Dancing Ledge, Tilly Whim, and Durlston Bay. Easier for operations was Studland Bay with its wide sandy bottom and ample areas of dense cover. Often, kegs were hidden temporarily under seaweed that had been dragged up the beach for fertiliser. From there the tubs were carried across the heath to Brand's Point, Greenland or Redhorn Quay and loaded into flat-bottom canoes, unsporting punt-gun platforms, to be rowed to the other side of the harbour. The closely watched entrance to the harbour at the Haven had to be avoided.

Six seized at Tyneham, 1834

Six Purbeck smugglers appeared at the Lent assize which opened at Dorchester on 14 March 1834. They were aged between sixteen and thirty-five, and their entry in the "Calendar of Prisoners at Dorchester Prison", now at Dorset Record Office, reads:

Committed by the Reverend Nathaniel Bond and the Reverend George Pickard, Junior, charged on the oaths of Lieutenant Henry John Carr, Chief Officer of the Coast Guard stationed at Kimmeridge in the Isle of Purbeck, and others, at a place called Gadcliffe [Gad Cliff, above the appropriately named Brandy Bay] in the parish of Tyneham, in the said Isle of Purbeck on the evening of the 31 January, they being then and there assembled in order to be aiding and assisting in the illegal landing, running or carrying away, prohibited goods. – Warrant dated 10 February 1834. – *Death recorded.*

That record is misleading: at the Midsummer sessions on 1 July that year their death sentences were commuted to hard labour for a year in each case. Philip Draper told me in 1969 about a smugglers' hiding hole constructed at the west end of Gad undercliff, near Pondfield Cove, which he had been shown by a Worbarrow fisherman in the 1930s.

Smuggler stoned to death on Worbarrow Beach

Llewellyn Pridham, in *The Dorset Coastline*, recorded a story about a smuggler who was stoned to death at Cow Corner, the western end of Worbarrow beach: "There is a queer legend about this lonely piece of shore, which only serves to enhance its eeriness. A smuggler took to his heels when beset by the revenue men, and not knowing that the beach ended up against a precipice ran like the wind, followed much slower by the officers of the law who knew that they already possessed him. Turning at bay he was forced to take to the sea, where he was stoned till he died. The story goes on to relate that at the waning of the moon, during the quietude of the night, sounds of strife can still be heard and half choked screams."

Worbarrow's smuggling Millers

The last person who remembered the smugglers of Purbeck was Walter Miller of Chaldon Herring who was born in Rose Cottage on the Burning Cliff at Ringstead, 24 June 1890. He looked back for me, in 1971, to those figures of the past:

My grandfather, Joseph Miller, was born at Worbarrow. He died at West Lulworth in about 1911, aged about seventy-eight. All the Miller family were smugglers before the Crimean War. The landowners and gentry smiled at this as it wasn't considered a crime. If they were caught with their gear and their boat and all that, they had six months imprisonment, but not hard labour.

One of my great uncles did his time at Dorchester. He was unlucky to be caught, and when he came out of jail, he was met by the squires and whatever and was taken to the Kings Arms for a good meal; because cellars were getting low, you see. They condoned it in a way.

We have a grapple, used to grapple up the barrels when they were sunk at the bottom. Grandfather, Joseph, had to give up smuggling in 1854 because the Russian war broke out and all the coastguards were called up to serve in the Baltic fleet. Then they recruited all the smugglers to be extra-men, as they called them: that is, coastguards.

Old Harry Vye and my grandfather and a few more had to sit on the cliff and watch for the smugglers who didn't come! They couldn't risk doing the two jobs at once. That's George Begg [he pointed to a photograph]. He didn't like me; he used to think I was too mischief-full or something. There was a story of a coastguard who accused a smuggler of doing something, pulled out a revolver and shot this man. What comforted the smugglers was that this coastguard was called up to the fleet in the Russian war, got frostbite – and both his ears fell off. They said it was retribution.

George Begg was at Ringstead and had a boat of his own and went to Cherbourg to get a load. He had a twenty-two foot *lerret* [Dorset dialect word for a type of fishing boat] and built a house at Ringstead to conceal it. The boat wasn't on the beach: when he wanted to he just had to slip it out and go to France. He was a clever old fellow. He used to wear those white trousers when I was a boy: I suppose he died about eighty-five in 1898. Dr Good from Dorchester came twice and said he was finished, but George Begg got up and went to sea again. He had another bout and this time the doctor said: "I think he will do." He died! Dr Good was wrong in all his predictions. It didn't enhance my father's opinion of doctors. "No bloody good," he used to say. Good for nothing, that lot were.

These memories cover the closing years of the smuggling trade. Another account survives from the opening period of the history of organised illegal importation of spirits and wines, tobacco, pepper and other taxable luxury items. By 1727, the state's annual income from excise duty had reached nearly £2,500,000. Already the business of evasion was far more successful and sophisticated than the inadequate machinery established to ensure that duties were paid.

George Wellstead operated fishing boats at Worbarrow in the nineteenth century and was the major Wareham dealer in shellfish.

Five Worbarrow coastguards drowned 1865

On a Saturday afternoon in March 1865 five men of Worbarrow coastguard station set sail to return to Weymouth in a galley laden with stores. They passed a gale warning, displayed from Admiral Fitzroy's signal opposite Weymouth Telegraph Station, forecasting southerly winds. These caught them about three miles from their base, when they were a mile off Lulworth Cove, and a watchman saw the sea strike the galley and sink her "like a stone". There were no survivors.

Worbarrow rescue on Christmas Day, 1883

The Great Western Railway's steamer *South of Ireland* terminated her Christmas Day cruise in 1883 on the rocks on the edge of Worbarrow Bay. Appropriately for the date all aboard were saved. The rocks had completely holed the vessel and she became a total wreck.

The *Palala*, a 1,408-ton steamer, was wrecked on the Kimmeridge Ledges on 15 May 1886 though all the passengers and crew were also rescued on that occasion. To the west of Kimmeridge Bay, the projecting shelf of Broad Bench claimed the schooner *Liberty* on 25 September 1868 and the smack *Ceres* on 21 March 1886. The brigantine *Wild Wave* was a total loss on Peveril Ledge on 23 January 1875. Another brigantine, *Commodore*, was a total wreck on Encombe Ledge on 18 August 1877.

Sometimes the sea released its catch, as with the schooner *Minnie* which was hard on Kimmeridge Ledges on 11 January 1890 but rescued by a decent tide. Likewise when the Russian sailors of the 3,512-ton steamer *Cerera* rammed the rocks a mile east of St Alban's Head on the night of 14 April 1907, they were fortunate to be pulled clear.

'When you see an old man, ask him all you can'

Walter Miller, whose memories of smugglers are printed a couple of pages back, also told me about the legitimate old-time fishing industry of Purbeck, Lulworth and Ringstead. He was once advised by his friend the writer Llewelyn Powys: "When you see an old man, ask him all you can." This I did when I was with Miller and he explained how the old fishermen lived and worked by pot-fishing in the shallow offshore waters:

Lobsters used to be caught more than crabs, as those change their skins and are slim before they do so. The saying is that crabs are good when there is an 'r' in the month. But in May, June and July they aren't much good.

There was fifteen fishermen at Lulworth, and now there's only two. There were around six at Worbarrow. There was Jack and Tom, and another called Tarry and his mate, and then there was old Charlie. All were one family originally but Henry Miller, the last one, had two sons, Jack and Tom, and both died during the war after the occupation [by the military in 1943].

At Ringstead the catch was rowed to Weymouth. That at Worbarrow was taken by fishmongers who used to come down over Tyneham hill from Wareham. They came the same to Lulworth. Father and them, when they couldn't come, they carried their catch on their backs to Weymouth and that was never considered any trouble. The fishmongers at Wareham, when they had too much, put what was over into a packing case. The lobsters were live with seaweed over them. They put them on a fast passenger train to London and they were sold at Billingsgate.

When mother had two lobsters, a pound-and-a-half, she would cook them, cool them down, put them in a basket and I'd take them and sell them at ninepence a pound. That made your mouth water! Everyone would have a feed of lobster sometimes. Good sirloin beef was then eightpence a pound. Visitors would come down and get the lobsters fresh, cooked on spatches.

All these fishermen were rabbit catchers in the winter. They had to because you couldn't make a living out of fishing alone, as you couldn't earn enough; there wasn't enough gear. Sixty pots was as much as you could do. Now they work four hundred and the Lulworth Grounds, a huge triangular shape off Lulworth, is prime fishing. They come up from Swanage and down from Brixham. But the lobsters aren't there now and we consider it's overfished. In the old days everything had a chance to live.

Remembering Victorian Tyneham

The twentieth century's last link with Victorian Tyneham was Margaret Bond who wrote to me on 8 February 1987 from Culliford House in Dorchester where she was about to celebrate her 95th birthday. She was the third daughter of William Bond who had owned Tyneham from 1898 until his death in 1935. Her memories, therefore, are now quite unique. "Like so many other things one did not bother to think of whys and wherefores until all the older generations have gone. Now I am the last of my generation of Tyneham and Creech Grange Bonds."

She lived in Tyneham House until the war made its first demands in about 1941 when the Royal Air Force erected a coastal radar station on the ridge east of Tyneham Cap. The Bonds went to live in the next house on the estate, the Gardener's Cottage, between Tyneham House and Tyneham Farm.

Margaret Bond was brought up to believe that as landowners her family had duties and obligations as well as rights. Her father had made the Ocean Seat, high on the side of Tyneham Cap and with a superb view of the Channel shipping: "The original one was exactly in the position you describe. It was where the footpath which ran all along the top of Gad Cliff from Worbarrow left the hilltop and went winding round the lower part of Tyneham Cap to descend to South Tyneham and South Egliston.

"When my father succeeded his uncle in 1898 there was a seat already in place. We thought it was for the uncle's two sisters who used to be taken up there in a carriage, all through the Great Wood. Ladies in those days did not possess walking out shoes! Some time after we went to live there, my father had a really superior shelter built of Purbeck stone, high enough at the back and sides to keep off wind, and on the open side, a flat-topped stone wall the right height to sit on comfortably if the wooden seat was full up."

The family sent one of its sons to South Africa in 1899

for the Boer War: "When my eldest brother returned from South Africa after a terrible time shut up in Ladysmith very badly wounded, my parents decided to give the church an organ as a thanksgiving. Before that there was only a harmonium.

"Then came the question of heating, damp being very bad for the organ. I suppose there was no kind of heating at all, though one old resident told me she believed some people brought to church with them small oil lamps to stand at the side of their pew.

"A hideous but efficient black iron 'tortoise' stove, with a black iron pipe all up the wall and out through the roof, was put in; it stood in the corner on the left-hand side between the nave and the chancel."

In 1911, beside the village water tap at the steps to the churchyard, Margaret Bond planted the oak which replaced an old and dangerous elm tree which her father had felled.

I had mentioned one of the villagers who was old then: "The reference to dear Louis Stickland brings back memories of him even though he died as long ago as the 1914-18 war. He and his son, Will, though fishermen by trade, were also very clever craftsmen. As well as building boats in their large boathouse at Charnel, on the west side of Kimmeridge Bay, they were expert builders in stone.

"In 1900 my father wanted to have a shed in the Lower Horseclose, near Shoemaker's Lane, as there was no shelter for young cattle in that part of the straggling farm. Louis and his son not only built the very substantial open-fronted shed but they opened a quarry near the top of Shoemaker's Lane to provide the material.

"When I remember Louis he was a regular attender at morning service in Tyneham church. Though much nearer Kimmeridge where he lived – his one-storey house was at the lower end of South Egliston gwyle – it was in Tyneham parish. On Sundays he always dressed in a black frock coat and wore a strange kind of black top hat. He chose the hard way to reach Tyneham, by coming up the gwyle and then climbing the quite stiff side of Tyneham Cap to the Ocean Seat to slope down outside the Great Wood to pass Tyneham Farm. Going home he always took the easier way, up the road and along the top of the Knap to Shoemaker's Lane and so over the hill to Egliston again.

"We never knew why he always came the hard way."

Similar recollections have come to me from a collection of Tyneham ex-residents, descendants and admirers who are now dispersed across Britain and the globe. The latest batch recall Worbarrow fishermen such as Jack Miller at Sea Cottage and Tom Miller and his father, Henry Miller, in Hill Cottage. A cottage in the valley there was the home of Beattie and Winnie Mintern. Their smallholding supplied the valley with milk, butter and eggs. The butter-making was carried on in a thatched room at the end of the house. On the opposite side of the stream stood Rose Cottage and the last person to live there was Arthur Stockley and his family. Nearby, in Fern Hollow, lived Charles and Harriette Miller. Reggie Ware, a soldier of the Great War, lived in the range of cottages that are now reduced to a few walls on the right of the track into Worbarrow from Tyneham Gwyle.

A particular gem of location, tucked immediately beneath the Purbeck Hills on the Flower's Barrow hill-fort side of Baltington Farm, has a name to match. It is one of those placenames that are so evocative of the Dorset up-along and down-along countryside but which the Ordnance Survey balked at recording because they sound so rustic. "Up Under Barrow" was the local name for this cottage — it sums up a different world that we have lost.

Weld-Blundell allows pitching of Lulworth Camp, 1916

The gunnery school of the Royal Armoured Corps remains firmly established on the edge of Lulworth Cove. Cottages and farmsteads at Tyneham are ruinous and mostly open to the sky. Time, and the inroads of this century, stopped abruptly many years ago, and it is a jungle that has taken their place. The resultant tangle can look futuristic at times with cobwebs moistened by the sea fog, lined along discarded missile guidance wire draped through the trees.

The first stage in the elimination of this coastal community came in 1916 when the War Office chose land at Lulworth for testing the world's first tanks. Weld-Blundell, the owner of Lulworth Castle, allowed the army to pitch its tents on the site of the present Lulworth Camp and the tank trials were carried out on the downland slopes of Bindon Hill between the Cove and Arish Mell.

The experimental unit with the first tanks was the Heavy Branch Machine Gun Corps, at Elveden in Suffolk. They moved to Dorset in 1916, as one of the first officers recalled in 1938:

> Wool, Bovington and Lulworth Cove were chosen for the headquarters of the Corps, and it was for camps near those delightful Dorset villages that we left Elveden late in November 1916. There we found a hive of activity, and recruits in plenty. Apparently infantry battalion commanders had been circularised and asked to recommend their "most intelligent men, particularly those with some mechanical knowledge".
> Needless to say, such a request produced the inevitable result, and we found that the new drafts consisted not infrequently of agricultural labourers and men with interesting crime sheets. But a year later I would not have exchanged one of these men for the most highly skilled mechanic in the country.
> At Wareham in 1918 there came back one faint echo of the heroic beginnings of the war, faint indeed as Roland's hour. A company of German prisoners and a company of Conscientious Objectors were put to work on the same fatigue. An hour later the German contingent arrived at Brigade Headquarters with a manifesto which read: "We, the undersigned, being good men and true, who have borne with our English brothers the burdens of war, see no reason why we should be so disgraced as to have to work with these cowards."
> The C.O. was amused and sympathetic. The Germans were given the afternoon off. They clicked heels happily, bowed with Teutonic dignity, and marched off with vast contented smiles.

'Tanks crawling like huge tortoises'

Jack Lawley, the son of a range warden near Wareham, recalled for me his first sight of tanks in Dorset: "Then something new appeared on the heath around us, crawling about like huge tortoises. They were a new weapon of war, the tank. They would crawl up the hills, then dip their noses down and crawl down again."

After they were tested in the sparsely populated Dorset heaths, the world's first tanks rolled into battle on the Somme in 1916. "A pretty mechanical toy," was Kitchener's derisory comment. In this the war lord summed up the general establishment reaction. The tank concept was pushed on to a reluctant War Office by Lieutenant-Colonel Ernest Swinton, serving not as a soldier but an official war correspondent, and who had written fiction under the pseudonym Backside-Forethought.

He had his invention rejected and then the idea was revived – this time in the unlikely surroundings of the Admiralty, where it had come to the notice of a former war correspondent, Winston Churchill. Never at a loss for a suitable name to disguise something that had no earthly relevance to his department, Churchill formed a "Landships Committee".

Nautical names were also found for the body of the machine, which was called the "hull", and to describe the thing itself which (after rejection of "cistern") became "tank". The army came back into the development programme which also received some timely royal patronage. King George V rode round the grounds of Lord Salisbury's Hatfield Park in a tank on 8 February 1916. To make the course a little more taxing, a ten foot trench had been dug and a four foot vertical obstacle prepared. The tank cleared both and impressed virtually everyone except Lord Kitchener. The King knew a good toy when he saw one and suggested that a large number in the army would be a great asset.

There were similar mixed reactions on the Front. When

Major-General John Fuller saw his first tank he thought it was "a very graceful machine with beautiful lines" and that in use it would prove to be "an armoured mechanical horse". Of the first one hundred tanks, forty-nine went into action on 15 September 1916 and three from D-Company achieved the historically symbolic moment, which was witnessed from the air: "A tank is walking up the High Street of Flers with the British Army cheering behind."

The greatest success for the Tank Corps was on 19 August 1917. A decision had been taken that a string of pillboxes at St Julien had to be knocked out. Their walls were of reinforced concrete, more than three feet thick, and it was thought that the action would cost a thousand casualties. Instead the tanks went in first, followed by the infantry, under a smoke screen and without any preliminary bombardment. There were only two British deaths.

On 20 November 1917 a massed force of 350 tanks led by Brigadier-General Hugh Elles (right at the front in "Hilda" with the new Tank Corps banner flying from an ash stick) smashed through every line of trenches in the German front. It was the first time this had been achieved since the stalemate of trench warfare had begun. But the War Office estimated that such a breakthrough would take five months and £20,000,000 of ammunition. So no one followed through the breach.

There had to be a British propaganda cover-up. In this field the War Office often had more talent than they ever showed for fighting. They excelled themselves and produced a German hero who had halted the British advance. Never before had the British press been allowed to admit there were any brave Germans, and yet here was a British witness saying with War Office blessing: "I came to a German field battery, every gun out of action except one. By this was lying a single German officer, quite dead. In front of him were five tanks which he had evidently succeeded in knocking out single-handed with his gun. A brave man." Also a mythical man. The whole story was invented.

It was a story that was put forward by the reactionaries

for the rest of the war as a reason for abandoning the tank programme. Kitchener could no longer join in as he went down with the cruiser *Hampshire*, which struck a mine in the North Sea. Tank tactics on the Front became over-restrained with a general policy of dispersal. By the end of the war the Germans had their own tanks and similar capabilities – the British line was broken whenever it was attacked by tanks. The French too had their tanks, though hardly a great contribution to the war effort, and they were attractively dismissed by Fuller as "a kind of kitchen range on tracks, unblushingly useless".

Tanks won the decisive battle of the Great War at Amiens on 8 August 1918, tearing a gap eleven miles wide through the German lines. The Kaiser said that evening: "It is very strange that our men cannot get used to tanks."

Locals put in pens to stop them seeing tanks

Nelson Thomson, a Purbeck quarryman retired at Langton Matravers when I interviewed him in 1971, looked back to 1916, when he was a young shepherd at Lulworth for Alan Budden of Burngate Farm:

When they used to bring the tanks over from Bovington they used to shut us behind screens of hurdles or take us away so that we couldn't see them. They put an army control all along the roads and if anybody were within sight they used to put them off. It didn't make any difference because, when we were at Lulworth, the tanks was going along the road and firing there – and we was working there.

What I used to have to do was to take the sheep down on to the range from five o'clock to nine o'clock in the morning and then they did start firing and I had to bring them back. Then at two o'clock I'd bring them down, some days, from two to three o'clock and then back again. And then from six o'clock to eight o'clock in the evening. One time there I can remember a military policeman came out and started chasing me: I had sheep and troops and everything all mixed up together out of the square, opposite from where their tanks was.

When Lulworth Camp started it was all tents. They were sleeping under canvas. I can remember when the post office at Lulworth got hit with a shell. I don't know whether it was 1916 but there was an awful disturbance about it. Two shells went adrift somewhere – they said they ricocheted – and the post office and one of the houses got hit. The shells came from the tanks firing at the tank range at Lulworth.

St Andrews Farm is a seventeenth century stone building that stands on the south edge of Lulworth Camp. The Thomson family moved into it just two months before the camp was established. They were the first of the two hundred families evicted to create the Government's Lulworth and East Holme Ranges across 7,500 acres of the finest scenery in Dorset.

"We had very short notice to get out from there," Nelson remembered. "It was twelve o'clock midnight when we went away from that farm and went down to Coombe Keynes to a man named Mr. Ford."

Tyneham's dead of the Great War

A marble tablet in Tyneham church records the parish's Great War dead – Henry Balson, Charles Job Cleall, Harry and John Holland, William Meech and Bertram Taylor – with these words: "All men must die. It is only given to the few to die for their country."

'Most exquisitely beautiful stretch of the Wessex coast'

The tank brought the taste of advance to the stagnant warfare of the trenches. At home it brought defeat for the remote and insular peoples of the heath and hills of the Isle of Purbeck. In 1923 the War Department tired of its short lease over the land at Lulworth and applied to purchase the ranges. The first counter attack against the Government was launched by the Daily Mail:

> The assault on Lulworth Cove is of all those vandalistic enterprises the most inexcusable. The intention is to establish a tank gunnery school there. The Daily Mail has always supported the cause of the tank against the "bow and arrow" school at the War Office but we feel it is really preposterous to tell the British public that the only range suited for tanks is the most exquisitely beautiful stretch of the Wessex coast.
> A little investigation would prove that alternative sites can be

found without any difficulty. If the War Office does not show itself reasonable the House of Commons will have to intervene to save the threatened area from its assailants.

Blunder puts Lulworth Cove inside ranges

S.P.B. Mais reported in the Daily Graphic:

Lulworth Cove itself was originally included in the scheme. So little do the authorities know of the country that when it was pointed out to them that their western boundary extended to a point nine hundred feet west of a beauty spot at least as famous and often visited as Clovelly they said that "west" was a misprint for "east".

Judged from the point of view of fair play, it is questionable morality to hire by force a plot of ground which was already prospected as an eligible site for a seaside resort, turn it into a wilderness, and then offer to buy it at wilderness rates. Not only is the area covered by the tanks turned from an artists' paradise into a scapegoats' hell, but the actual property of Lulworth Castle becomes valueless. They could not have hit upon a worse plot of ground from every point of view. More and more it is becoming difficult for the townsman in search of a holiday to find some place that is both beautiful and quiet. The stretch of coast between Swanage and Lulworth is absolutely unspoilt.

No one is going to take a holiday in country where his way is constantly being barred owing to gun practice. Even now sentries demand passes before you are allowed over Bindon Hill. The danger area, by an amazing lack of foresight, includes the only fossil forest in Britain. Geologists and their pupils swarmed there. Now they will not be allowed even to see it.

The fishermen of Lulworth depend largely for a living on their lobster pots: if they go in an easterly direction they have to be back before nine in the morning. They can no longer shelter in Mupe's [all the old fishermen called it "Mupe's" rather than "Mupe"] Bay when they are unable to make Lulworth.

'Even the Huns never did this'

One of the fishermen told Mais: "I fought for this bit of land and when I come home they try to starve me out of it." Weld-Blundell, lord of the manor of Lulworth, put the matter in stronger terms. "Even the Huns," he said with fury, "never did a thing like this."

Lulworth Cove was then described in holiday propaganda as the "English Bay of Naples" and Mais seemed to have been the first person to make the pun about "collecting shells on a Dorset beach". Another kind of seashell: "It is not a game that I recommend to the many boy scouts and girl guides who are in camp nearby."

The Bournemouth Daily Echo reported on 30 November 1923 that not only was the future of the tank ranges under consideration but the War Office had been offered an alternative site on the other side of Lulworth Cove:

> Up to the present the War Office has made no announcements to relieve public suspense regarding its intentions for the future of Lulworth Cove.
>
> At this week's meeting of the Dorset County Council it was reported that no reply had been received to the protest of the council against the proposal to establish the Tank Gunnery School permanently at East Lulworth, and the only information available for the county authority was a statement that it is possible that the Army Council will not press the question of the purchase of the site but will continue to lease it.
>
> Lord Shaftesbury, the Lord Lieutenant of the County, could go no further than that, and the county council, equally with those people all over the country who wish to see our beauty spots preserved, must possess themselves in patience until the War Office thinks proper to give some indication of its attitude.
>
> The principal reason advanced for suggesting that the War Office may not purchase the site was, in the opinion of experts in the tank arm of the service, that the obvious line of development of the tank is in the direction of heavier armament and that with heavier guns being used the Lulworth range might prove inadequate. There is another point that is always worth bearing in mind – that is that the War Office has an alternative site offered them on the west side of the cove which would not interfere with the famous beauty spot.

The owner of Lulworth was joined by Thomas Hardy, Lord Shaftesbury and Sir Alfred Fripp in his struggle against the War Office plan to acquire permanently 973 acres of land between Lulworth Cove and Arish Mell. The tanks won.

'West' said to be mistake for 'east'

It was explained at the public inquiry into the 1923-24 proposals that there had been a clerical error in the setting out of the western boundary, caused by the insertion of the word "west" instead of "east" and it had therefore been "incorrectly assumed" by the press and public that Lulworth Cove itself was included. The boundary, the War Office continued, should have been specified as running to the east of the Cove, so that the range included Bindon Hill, and the firing would be infrequent and would consist mainly of light machine gun fire and "that as little inconvenience as possible would be caused to the public, the footpaths being allowed to be used on bank holidays, Saturdays, Sundays and special occasions and that suitable approved bye-laws would be drawn up; and on these occasions opposition was withdrawn".

Exactly the same offering would deflate the 1967-76 Tyneham campaign. Whitehall simply pulls out the appropriate contingency plan for dealing with this sort of thing.

The second stage of War Office encroachment at Lulworth had been surreptitiously achieved, but the people had been promised a future without further war. By this time there was a scrap heap of abandoned tanks on the Dorset heath to the north of Bovington Camp. In 1924 Rudyard Kipling visited Bovington and complained that no one appreciated the historic significance of these tanks and as a result two were put into a shed the following year. They were "Little Willie", the world's first tank, and "Mother", the first fighting version. Each weighed twenty-eight tons. Others soon joined them.

Rector rails against Tyneham's phone box

The remains of one of the early telephone kiosks, a white concrete affair, stand outside the Post Office where Wilson Coombes erected it in the 1920s. He told me he faced a tirade of abuse from the rector who resented the innovation. This would long ago have been replaced by a red metal box had peace returned to the valley. Tyneham school closed on 24 March 1932. This was ordered by the Board of Education "owing to the small number of pupils and urgent need for economy".

Stage three of the expansion of the Lulworth ranges was carried out in 1939 when the coming of a new war removed the necessity for the niceties of public consultation. The range bye-laws were altered to include a larger danger area and the public was totally excluded from the area. The eastern boundary of the new range lay on the east side of Arish Mell (instead of the west) so that this little bay which had been so popular with picnickers and courting couples through the 1930s was forbidden territory for the first time. The tank collection at Bovington was broken up, literally, with a few being spared for use as stationary pillboxes.

War comes to Tyneham

Tyneham, at the outbreak of hostilities, was an ordinary little community, exceptional only in that it did not have a public house. There had been none in the village itself though Thomas Spencer was recalled as a "beer retailer" in the fishermen's hamlet of Worbarrow for the third quarter of the nineteenth century, when John Lidderdale was master of the Coast Guard Station.

In those days, Worbarrow also had the only local shop, which was run by Joseph Miller. Indeed, when the lobster trade was flourishing, Worbarrow generated most of the area's activity.

By the 1880s, however, the village started to assert itself, with Mrs Ann Mores as shopkeeper in what became the Post Office. Harry Barnes ran it during the Great War. Mrs Edith Herd was postmistress in the 1930s.

In the heart of the valley, there was an oak beginning to mature near the south-east corner of the churchyard wall. It had been planted in 1911, for the coronation of King George V. Beneath it, recessed in stone, the village tap and trough would soon be dry. Not that the Biblical inscription, from John's gospel, chapter 4, verses 13 and 14, looked upon water as merely a temporal convenience: "WHOSEVER DRINKETH OF THIS WATER SHALL THIRST AGAIN: BUT WHOSOEVER DRINKETH OF THE WATER THAT I SHALL GIVE HIM SHALL NEVER THIRST; OUT OF THE WATER THAT I SHALL GIVE HIM SHALL BE IN HIM A WELL OF WATER SPRINGING UP INTO EVERLASTING LIFE."

On the outbreak of war, Sunday, 3 September 1939, Mrs Gwendoline Driscoll was the shopkeeper at the Post Office (telephone Kimmeridge 221). Rev Humphrey Churchill Money was at the Rectory (telephone Kimmeridge 219), having taken over on the death of Rev Edwin George Clifford Frend in 1937. Rev Christopher Campbell Sharpe, inducted in 1927, seems to have been the rector who objected to Wilson Coombes installing the telephone box outside the Post Office, though it could have been his predecessor, Rev Frederick de la Poer Beresford.

At Tyneham House, owner in residence was (William) Ralph Garneys Bond JP (telephone Kimmeridge 223), who inherited the estate on the death of his father, William Henry Bond JP.

Walter Case Smith was at Tyneham Farm. Albert Longman was farming Baltington, as he had for several decades. Herbert John House was the farmer at North Egliston. Albert Ernest Cranton was at Lutton Farm, between North Egliston and Steeple, the next village. All concentrated on dairying.

Sarah Minton ran a smallholding at Worbarrow. As for the "private residents" of the directories, listing those with a touch of class, there was Lieutenant-Commander Godfrey E.H. House RN, retired at South Egliston (telephone Kimmeridge 216) and Miss M. Ellis living in the Bungalow on the cliff-edge at Worbarrow Bay.

This was the line-up of personalities in the coastal valley during the phoney war, before it suddenly became the front-line with the fall of France in May 1940 and the

Luftwaffe's instant take-over of the Cherbourg peninsula, only seventy miles south-east. Initially it was a sea war with the English Channel barred to shipping as the Stukas dive-bombed anything that moved between Lyme Bay and the Isle of Wight. Then the Germans turned their attention landwards and the Battle of Britain raged through the hot summer of 1940.

CHURCHILL INSPECTS CHURCHILLS

Above and below: **Newly-introduced Churchill tanks were tested by the Gunnery Wing of the Armoured Fighting Vehicles School, at Lulworth Camp, in the autumn of 1941. They ridiculed the 39-ton tank's two-pounder gun as a 'peashooter'. Some had been refitted with six-pounders, giving much increased fire-power, by the time the massed ranks went on the move through the Arish Mell valley for the benefit of Prime Minister Winston Churchill on 6 April 1942. He reviewed them at Sea Vale Farm, on the Lulworth side of Flower's Barrow.**

Photographs: Rodney Legg collection

Tyneham Germans were first fliers to be taken prisoner

There was an up-beat moment in Tyneham's war. Two enemy fliers in a Messerschmitt Me110 were brought down on Povington Heath on the afternoon of 11 July 1940, survived the crash landing and became the first Germans to be taken prisoner in the Battle of Britain. Intercepted by Spitfires from RAF Warmwell, the wartime aerodrome in the Frome valley near Dorchester, they had flown at noon from Laval, via a refuelling stop at Dinard, and were among fighters escorting Junkers Ju87 Stuka dive-bombers in an attack on Channel shipping off Portland.

The two-engined aeroplane had twisted propellers and a dented underside but was otherwise undamaged. Its crewmen were Oberleutnant Gerhard Kadow, the pilot, and Gefreiter Helmut Scholz, gunner, of the 9th Staffel, Zerstörergeschwader 76 – 9 Squadron of Destroyer Group 76. Kadow was not only unhurt but remained fit and well throughout his long captivity and into retirement, telling his tale in the 1980s:

> I flew Me110 number 2N + EP, with my wireless operator and air gunner, Gefreiter Helmut Scholz. My squadron was stationed at Laval, and we flew from there to Dinard for refuelling and from Dinard to England at about 12.00 hours, noon.
>
> My squadron, together with two others, had orders to protect Ju87 Stuka dive-bombers, which would attack targets on the south coast of England in the vicinity of Portland.
>
> Before we started, our commander, Major Grabmann, told us that it was vital that no Stuka be lost. This meant a considerable risk to our lives.
>
> At the English coast I counted some twenty dark spots in the distance, somewhat higher than we were. I was certain they were RAF fighters, but couldn't recognise whether they were Hurricanes or Spitfires – but knew that our twin-engined machines were no match for these single-engined fighters.
>
> However, it was our duty to protect the Stukas, so that they could bomb unhindered. The main strength of the Me110 was the two 20mm cannons and four machine guns in its nose. I pressed the firing buttons and bullets flew like water out of a watering can towards the enemy. The closing speed was high,

POVINGTON HEATH

Right: **First prisoner of the Battle of Britain, Oberleutnant Gerhard Kadow. He was shot down on Povington Heath, Tyneham, on 11 July 1940.**

Below: **First of the many – the very first German casualty of the Battle of Britain to be brought down on land. A Messerschmitt Bf-110 of the 9th Staffel of Zerostörergeschwader 76 crash-landed on Povington Heath, in the parish of Tyneham. Seen from the north, in the vicinity of Povington Farm, under British guard. The line of Purbeck Hills is clearly visible in the distance, with Povington Hill (centre) and the slight dip at Lawford Sheard Gate (right) which led to Tyneham Village. 11 July 1940.**

Photographs: Rodney Legg collection

and at the last minute both I and my attacker had to break away to avoid a head-on collision. Whether I scored any hits or not, I don't know.

The next moment, two fighters were on my tail and had opened fire. Almost immediately both of my engines stopped and a return to the Continent was clearly impossible. The enemy saw his success and stopped shooting, but watched me from behind.

I flung off my cabin roof for a quick escape and hoped it would hit him. I ordered Helmut Scholz to do the same. He radioed that the mechanism to ditch his cabin roof would not operate as a result of bullet damage.

I couldn't bail out and leave Scholz to his fate, and for the same reason a ditching in the sea seemed unwise. The only alternative was a crash landing on British soil.

After we had landed I found I could not leave my cockpit – a high explosive bullet had hit my seat, causing a big hole. The torn aluminium "fangs" around the hole had nailed themselves through my parachute pack and tunic on to my flesh.

I pulled myself forward, and suddenly was free. I left the aircraft and smashed the cabin roof of my gunner so that he could get out. He was hurt only by shell splinters. The first thing to do was destroy the aircraft. We didn't have a self-destruct charge, so I opened the fuel caps and tried to ignite the petrol with the muzzle flash from my pistol. I fired eight shots, but had no success. In hindsight, this was just as well, otherwise the aircraft would have exploded and killed us.

Tyneham requisitioned by War Cabinet, 19 December 1943

The red flags at the range boundary were now almost at the edge of the parish of Tyneham. There, in 1940, local magistrate Ralph Bond formed the Tyneham Home Guard with himself as platoon commander. He made what he thought would be his major contribution to the war effort in 1941 when the Royal Air Force requisitioned Tyneham House as the support facilities for a coastal radar station that was being set up on the ridge to the east of Tyneham Gap. The Bonds moved into the Gardener's Cottage between Tyneham House and Tyneham Farm. But a further price had to be paid.

The British and American armies, not the Germans, would bring the Second World War into every inch of

Tyneham valley on 19 December 1943.

All 3,003 acres of the parish of Tyneham, inhabited by a scattered population of about two hundred and fifty, and other land beneath Dorset's Purbeck Hills were evacuated by direct order from Winston Churchill's War Cabinet. Local councils were not allowed to question the correctness of the decision and censorship prevented any mention in the press of the requisition of the Purbeck training area. Never for one moment were the Tyneham area inhabitants led to believe that their evacuation was other than a temporary measure necessary for winning the war.

The whole of south Dorset became an armed camp in the spring of 1944, with thousands of men and vehicles, most of them American. Lulworth and Tyneham were assigned to the Sherman tanks of the Second Armoured Divison, the backbone of V Corps of the First United States Army – codenamed Force O (for Omaha) and tasked to take what would be the bloodiest of the Normandy beachheads in Operation Overlord. Theirs was the D-Day armada that sailed from Portland and Weymouth and touched the shore of occupied France at 06.34 hours on 6 June 1944.

'You have every right to return to the property'

All the Tyneham tenants were informed by the War Department land agent that, if they wished, their tenancies would be maintained. The notice served on each of them contained the following words:

"This means that when the War Department has no further use for the property and it is handed back, you have every right to return to the property. It should not be assumed by you that, because the War Department has turned you out, you lose your right of occupying the premises again."

Even though no mention of the Tyneham takeover was permitted in the press, anyone could have sensed the truth from the auction columns of the Dorset County Chronicle on 2 December 1943. Western Purbeck sounded like a disaster zone. Auctioneers Henry Duke and Son offered 313 dairy cows and bulls, nine working horses, 71 sheep, 33 pigs, 167 poultry, four Fordson tractors, and over 700 separate lots of farm implements from the Tyneham valley alone. The farmers were fleeing:

"Tyneham Farm, Tyneham, for Mr S.G. Churchill, quitting.
"Lutton Farm, Steeple, for Mr A.E. Cranton, quitting.
"Baltington Farm, Tyneham, for Mr A.J. Longman, quitting.
"North Egliston Farm, Tyneham, for Mr H.J. House, quitting."

On the other side of the Purbeck Hills there was a similar pattern of tragedy. Thomas Ensor & Son announced dispersal sales at West Creech Farm(for R.C. Cake); Povington Farm (T.W. Wrixon); Searleys Farm, Povington (Arthur Cooper); Jiggiting Corner, Povington (J. Cooper); Weld Arms Farm, East Lulworth (Mrs B. Bonham); The Cat, East Lulworth (Mrs S.P. Damen); Whiteway Farm, East Lulworth (H.J. Sampson); Broadmoor Farm, West Creech (H.C. George); White Hall Farm, West Creech (W. Cake); Rookery Farm, West Creech (Frank Cranton); Hurst Mill Farm, West Creech (A.E. Swain).

There was a sad note at the end of the lists: "The Auctioneers wish to draw special attention to the before mentioned Sales and sincerely trust that all farmers from over a wide area will endeavour to attend as many as possible to assist in the dispersal of the stock on offer, all of which is thoroughly recommended by the Auctioneers."

'Help towards winning the war with a good heart'

Frank Cranton was the lucky evacuee as he was able to secure another farm, keep most of his stock and cancel the "away-going" sale at Lutton. Miss Helen Taylor was evicted from Tyneham and moved to a council home at Corfe Castle. She preserved the eviction notice which was signed by Major-General Charles Harvey Miller of Southern Command on 16 November 1943 and stated: "The Government appreciate that this is no small sacrifice which you are asked to make, but they are sure you will give this further help towards winning the war with a good heart."

Many of the elderly villagers, like fisherman Jack Miller of Sea Cottage, Worbarrow failed to survive their uprooting and died before the war was over.

John Charlton wrote to me from Oxfordshire in 1968 when he saw Jack Miller's Sea Cottage at Worbarrow pictured in ruins in the Dorset County Magazine: "I wonder what has happened to Miggy and her husband with their stuffed cat who used to live in the cottage on the front of your first issue."

Marriage register stamped 'Cancelled'

The young were able to adapt and make new lives for themselves. Sarah Braisley lived at Egliston in a secluded valley above Kimmeridge Bay. She was the last girl to marry in Tyneham's mediaeval parish church, on 23 May 1943. Below this final entry, the marriage register, which spanned nearly 150 years, was stamped twice with a blue oval "Cancelled".

"It was quite a wrench when we moved out. But it was for the good of the country. It was rather exciting in a way for me, but it affected my parents a lot. It meant selling everything."

Poppy Budden, her sister, was then eighteen years old. She emphasised: "We were given an understanding that we would move back there some day. Most people expected to go back. But I don't feel any bitterness about it and I look back on the years at Tyneham as a very happy time."

The reaction of Mrs S.B. White is different: "I find it too painful even to go back and look at Tyneham again. Members of my family are buried in the tiny churchyard and my mother's old homestead on Povington Heath can just boast a pile of stone, part of the chimney stack and a lonely and gruesome looking yew tree."

'We shall thank you for treating the village kindly'

As the last residents evacuated the valley they pinned a farewell notice to the church door: "Please treat the church and houses with care. We have given up our homes, where many of us have lived for generations, to help win the war to keep men free. We shall return one day and thank you for treating the village kindly."

The church held a special place in Tyneham hearts and would survive in better shape than the village, being left in the ownership of the Church Commissioners.

St Mary's is a delightful cross-shaped building, with a bellcote just off centre but no tower, on the original thirteenth century cruciform plan. Walls of that period survive in the north transept, including external buttresses at the outer corners, and the north side of the nave. Contemporary features include a double-lancet window and a roughly carved double-arched piscina.

Beside the piscina there would have been the altar for what was initially the chantry chapel for the Russel family of the mediaeval Tyneham House. The earliest monument to a valley-owning family is that for John Williams [died 1627] and wife Jane [1636], erected by grandson John Williams in 1641.

The next squirearchy is represented by the black marble tablet in an elaborate surround to Mrs Bond's faithful servant Elizabeth Tarrant who died in 1769 and had given thirty-four years of her life to looking after Tyneham House. The wooden wall panel with the text of verse nine of the 96th Psalm is also from the eighteenth century.

The rebuilt south transept, with its stone panel above the doorway in the east wall carved with the arms of the Bond family, dates from the time of Rev William Bond who was the rector from 1795 until his death, at the age of ninety-five, in 1852. The fourteenth century south porch, tucked away in a corner, was taken down and rebuilt at the west end of the nave, in a sympathetic restoration that preserves its charm. The Royal Commission on Historical Monuments gives the credit "for at least part of this work" to Christchurch architect Benjamin Ferry.

Writing in 1970, the Commission go on to say that "the chancel is modern". Turning to church historian Fred Pitfield's *Purbeck Parish Churches*, one finds it is the 1872 work of architect George Crickmay of Weymouth and builder John Wellspring of Dorchester. More modern still was the "handsome new organ" of 1902 which Mr and Mrs W.H. Bond presented as a thank-offering for the recovery of their son Algy [Lieutenant Algernon Bond], from a serious wound received during the siege of Ladysmith.

Perishable contents were dispersed after 1943. The organ went to Steeple. The pulpit, which had seventeenth century side panels, was taken to Lulworth Camp chapel. The church plate, notably a cup and cover-paten by Lawrence Stratford of Dorchester [1574], went to Kimmeridge.

Having survived years of neglect behind a tall barrier of barbed wire, from which it could be just glimpsed from the closest point outside the former Post Office, the church became a local museum in the late 1970s – though it is only accessible (at Ordnance Survey map reference SY 881 806) when the Lulworth Range Walks are open. That is generally the case most weekends, for the whole month of August, and over the Christmas holiday.

Viscount Hinchingbrooke MP denounces 'spoliation of our countryside'

Post-war opposition to the retention of the Purbeck Tank Gunnery Ranges by the War Office stretched across the political spectrum and was at an intensity that makes modern local affairs sound quite tame. South Dorset's Member of Parliament was Viscount Hinchingbrooke, Conservative, who had served in France in 1940 and afterwards on the General Staff of Home Forces. He made an uncompromising speech to the Society of Dorset Men gathered at their annual dinner in London's Connaught Rooms on 5 May 1947:

"The part of Dorset I love best, extending from Corfe to Lulworth, is bound like Andromeda to the rock. The War Office dragon is breathing its fire and smoke over her, and we, like Perseus, must go to her rescue.

"There were two occasions in history when the sons of Dorset rose in defence of her coasts. At the time of the Napoleonic menace, so wonderfully depicted by Thomas Hardy in *The Dynasts*, every man leapt to his allotted post in order to defend her shores, and again in September 1940, when the alarm was once more given. In both cases the alarm was unfounded. But we must not allow it to be said that Dorset men only move into action when the alarm is false.

"Today there is an urgent alarm – South Dorset is gradually being turned, by an insidious process, into a military encampment – and the project will be backed up by all the mercenary and commercial forces which come in its train. We must attempt some concrete action to prevent this going any further. We should make it the objective of this dinner, and indeed of county activities as a whole, to release our county as far as possible from military control.

"What is the use of a great standing army and fleets of aircraft if the source and inspiration of patriotism is lacking through the spoliation of our countryside?"

Hinchingbrooke, however, was to be no stranger to lost causes. In 1962 he succeeded his father as the tenth Earl of Sandwich but disclaimed the peerage for life in an attempt, which failed, to remain in the House of Commons. As president of the Anti-Common Market League he led the resistance to Britain joining the European Economic Community. It was as Victor Montagu that he retired to Mapperton Manor in the hills of west Dorset between Beaminster and Powerstock.

By 1947 there was a revival of interest in Lulworth and Tyneham's discarded tanks and those vintage specimens that had not been scrapped were gathered up again from the heaths and coast, where they had served as anti-invasion pillboxes, and put back into the museum at Bovington. "Little Willie" survived and so too did a reasonable spread of First World War tanks including specimens of Mark I, IV, V, VIII and IX. There is also a miniature British tank, the 14-ton "Whippet" dating from 1916, and a "Peerless" armoured car built in 1917. The Second World War had brought the museum a representative collection of foreign tanks as well.

Attlee Government accepts pledges were given

In December 1947 Clement Attlee's post-war Labour Government admitted in its command White Paper Number 7278:

> In the case of some of the proposed training areas particularly Stamford and the Purbeck tank gunnery school it has been, or may be represented, that pledges were given, or understood to be given, and it will not therefore be necessary to press the point at any public enquiry; at the same time for reasons given in earlier paragraphs, areas for practical training must be provided and it follows that if an area in respect of which a pledge was given were surrendered and a new area taken up, one result would be the eviction of residents in the new area for the benefit of those originally displaced.

That sealed the fate of Tyneham and the heathland hamlet of Povington on the other side of the Purbeck Hills. The Government freely admitted that promises of the land's return "at the end of the emergency" had been given. But Britain's extended firing ranges were part of the War Office's gains from the Second World War and it was not going to give them away. A public inquiry was duly held in 1948 and the War Minister, John Strachey, upheld "the national interest".

Ralph Bond, the last squire, 1880-1952

Ralph Garneys Bond, the last man to own Tyneham, died in 1952 at Moigne Combe, near Moreton railway station, shortly after receiving £90,000 compensation for the loss of his land. Eviction from the house which his family had owned since 1583 was an ironic climax to a life that is as much a cameo of that past as the deserted cottages. He was a representative of England's landed gentry and an upholder of its empire. Born during the exceptionally cold winter of 1880, Bond went through Eton and into the colonial service for a long term in Sudan. There in 1913 he shot a Dorcas gazelle with a head of world record size. Bond lived with his pets and servants, including faithful Said who came to him as a small boy and remained throughout his career. Later he became an expert naturalist, gave a giraffe to London Zoo, and retired to study the smaller fauna of Dorset.

He married more than twenty years after he left school, and as the last squire of Tyneham he left a memory of a kindly old man doing his best to protect his tenants from officialdom but accepting his own fate without bitterness. As administrator to the last, he succeeded his cousin, John Bond of Creech Grange, as chairman of Wareham bench which he left through deafness in his declining years, when the ruination of Tyneham "hurt him terribly".

Tyneham House 'ranks before any other in Purbeck', 1867

In 1867 one of his ancestors, Thomas Bond, had described Tyneham House as the finest country house in Purbeck: "In size and importance, as well as in solidity of masonry and general appearance, this house ranks far before any other ancient mansion now remaining in the Isle of Purbeck, though its aspect has been sadly marred externally by the introduction of sash windows on the ground floor which, however they may add to the comfort and convenience of the occupiers, are highly disfiguring to a building of this character."

Elizabethan main section demolished, 1968

Tyneham House is now a ruin that can only deteriorate further as it is totally abandoned and crumbles within the overshoot area of the Lulworth army ranges.

The main section of the Bond family's former home, its east side, was demolished in 1968. At the back of the ruins of the principal part of Tyneham House are the derelict remains of a fourteenth century hall with great oak beams and elaborate timber trusses supporting the roof. The hall was built by the Russel family and altered somewhat by Henry Williams in 1567. He came from Probus, Cornwall, to Hatch Beauchamp and then Tyneham, where he erected the great open fireplace in the mediaeval hall. Tyneham House then became one of the outstanding small country houses of Dorset. Its Elizabethan main section of 1583 was constructed in grey Purbeck stone, with neat mullions until high Victorian windows were inserted along the ground floor. The rooms looked out across lawns edged with palms and other semi-tropical plants that accepted the mild, moist microclimate of the valley. Beyond the lawns was an avenue of tall beech trees.

Woodwork from the house, principally carved wall panelling, was removed to the Dorset County Museum at Dorchester. In 1965 the Ancient Monuments Board received an exaggerated report of the house's collapse. Unfortunately, once attention had been drawn to Tyneham House, the process began that was to end in its demolition. The irony is that the sums involved would today be regarded at trivial and that a lesser building, structurally and architecturally, that stands nearby in the village, was rescued in the mid-1970s as a museum. The statement from the Ministry of Public Buildings and Works shows that at no stage did anyone consider the possibility that a decade later the position might be completely changed:

> The report by the Ministry's architect and inspector for the area showed that the main block of the house seemed to be

somewhat less severely damaged than had been feared, since the roof had not wholly collapsed, and the South-west Wing, containing the earliest work, although in a deplorable condition, partly collapsed internally, sodden, and covered with ferns and creepers, at least retained one bay of its timbered roof and its supports from ground level upwards, most of which appeared to be original. Damage was due to natural causes and had not been caused by shell fire.

A detailed estimate of the cost of preserving the building from further deterioration which included such things as clearance of vegetation and debris, formation of draining ditches to take away rain water, erection of a temporary roof and other coverings, closing up of door and window openings and strutting where required, amounted to the substantial sum of £8,000 – £2,500 for the South-west Wing; £300 for the East Porch; and £5,200 for the main house.

With the exception of a few odd days when access was possible it was only feasible to carry out such work during two brief periods of the year when the ranges are not in use – three weeks in August, and two in December. The condition of the building was such, however, that it was considered that if action was not taken very soon to preserve the more perishable part of the work, all would be lost except the masonry shell.

In these circumstances, it was felt that there were formidable difficulties in the way of preserving the building, and the Board eventually decided that salvage of the building as a whole would be an impossibility, and that the best that could be done was to allow certain features of the building which were capable of being dismantled and erected elsewhere to be removed from the site [such as arches, to Robin Cooke's Athelhampton Hall and Lord Southborough's Bingham Melcombe]. With the greatest regret, the rest of the fabric has had to be abandoned. The Ministry of Housing and Local Government, on whose list the house appears, are aware of the position.

The loss of Tyneham House is the greatest single blow that the historical heritage of Purbeck has suffered during this century. Other lesser buildings of the seventeenth century and later were also destroyed at Tyneham during the 1960s and 70s. The large nineteenth century rectory was burned down in 1966. The schoolhouse still had long rows of empty pegs but was ruinous until the military took down the walls to head-height in the name of conservation and safety. Tyneham Farm was reduced to a ruined shell and then demolished; Jack Miller's cottage is virtually nothing now; Worbarrow's other old cottages and the former coastguard station are nearly down to their foundations; houses at South Egliston are battered. The seventeenth century house and barn at Lutton are decaying. Only the church has been actively preserved and it was partially reroofed in 1969. The building seems to have been nearly hit by a shell as an area in the churchyard was soft and covered with new turf. It is claimed that one of the graves received a direct hit and had its bones exposed. Since then the church has received better care and is now newly restored as a museum of village life.

Older burial mounds, on the heath at Povington, were virtually destroyed in 1971. Thorn Barrow and three other Bronze Age round barrows dating from about 1800 BC had only recently been marked with metal star signs "to render identification by the military easier". This was intended to protect them from accidental damage as they were scheduled as an ancient monument by the Department of the Environment. One barrow stood ten feet high but all four were "badly damaged" by military action. Thorn Barrow became a tank-scoop, and the four mounds in barrow group 702 were written off by the Department of the Environment in 1971 as being damaged beyond saving and recommended for excavation.

Miss Joyce Melhuish at the Department of the Environment wrote to me in 1974 to say that of the two Bronze Age round barrows at Rings Hill, Arish Mell, "one is recorded as having been completely destroyed at some time between the date of scheduling [1962] and 1967".

The 'gwyles' – wooded glens

Jungle conditions have set in to the damper woods. Particularly attractive features of the landscape in the part of Tyneham parish south of the ridge are the *gwyles*. This is a Dorset dialect word given to wooded glens, though which flow small streams, near the coast. Inside the army ranges are Tyneham Gwyle, Lutton Gwyle and Egliston Gwyle. These secluded woods are decaying and in their present state the stench of the ground covering of wild garlic in spring is overpowering. David Trehane, at 83 in 1992, told me the origin of the word *gwyle*. It is from Cornwall, where it means wild or uncultivated ground, being introduced to Purbeck when the Williams family moved to Tyneham House from Probus in 1567.

96 miles of stopped-up paths

In 1960 when the Government took action to stop-up ninety-six miles of public paths inside the ranges, John Durrant-Lewis of Wareham and Purbeck Rural Council was instructed by his councillors to protest "that the council fails to see how it can be stated that it is necessary or expedient in the public interest that the public should be deprived for all time of rights over thirty-seven ways, which must have existed for centuries and which, at the present time, are of some minor inconvenience to the present temporary owners ..."

Those "present temporary owners", the War Office, gave Dorset County Council the following undertakings on 30 April 1962:

> a) that should the occasion arise when the ranges, or any part thereof, cease to be used for their present purposes and the necessity for a danger area from which the public are excluded has passed, the highways shall be restored for use by the public either along the original lines or along some other convenient lines to be agreed;
> b) that the War Office will not transfer East Holme and East Lulworth ranges or any part thereof to any other Government department except on the conditions that the transferee department gives an undertaking in the same terms;
> c) that the War Office will not dispose of the East Holme and East Lulworth ranges, or any part thereof, to any public authority, private person or body without first rededicating the rights of way either along the original lines or along some other convenient lines to be agreed, unless the fulfilment of this requirement is agreed between the War Office and the county, urban, rural and parish councils concerned to be unnecessary in the light of the circumstances then obtaining.

The continuing saga of the Tyneham affair is one where promises have always been plentiful. It would be difficult to put any such proposals to the "parish council concerned" as Tyneham is the only parish in Dorset which has a nil return in its register of electors.

'A promise given by the British Government turned out worthless'

Those pledges about Tyneham were not forgotten, and were repeated to a Ministry of Defence departmental committee on defence lands in 1971. But it was the fifth Marquess of Salisbury, nicknamed Bobbity, the Tory elder statesman who had been the Member of Parliament for South Dorset in 1943, who summed them up better than anybody. He made the only television speech of his life, for Granada's "World in Action" on 4 August 1969:

> For twelve years before the Second World War I was Member of Parliament for South Dorset and as such I came to know the Tyneham valley very well. Nothing could have been more charming, more peaceful or more remote than it was at that time: a little folded valley between the downs and the sea with a grey Elizabethan manor house and a church and a village to match; inhabited by families many of whose forebears had been there for centuries.
> And then the war came, and the War Office made an appeal to the people of Tyneham as a patriotic duty to leave their homes for the period of the emergency. And when the war came to an end and they thought they were at last being able to go back to their homes a message came from the War Office indicating that the promise that they had been given had no worth and that they could never return.
> By that time I had ceased to be the Member for South Dorset, but I felt that these Tyneham people had suffered a great injustice and I still think so. They had left their homes, trusting in a promise that had been given to them by the British Government and that promise had turned out to be worthless. And this breach of trust, as indeed it was, is something that I feel we should all be ashamed of and that is why I have said what I have said today, with a plea that this present Government will do what can be done, for nothing can quite restore the past, to right the wrong, which these harmless and good Englishmen have suffered.

The first official concession to be made inside the Lulworth ranges since the establishment of Lulworth Camp in

1916 did not take place until 1972. Dorset County Council then paid the army £550 for the cost of materials used to restore to the public its former legal right of access to the cycad tree-trunks of the Fossil Forest. The approach to this ledge above the sea, immediately east of Lulworth Cove, was "improved and made safe". The fossil trees are among the textbook sights of British geology but the Ministry of Defence was not as magnanimous as it may have seemed: the Fossil Forest never had an access problem as scientific students always slipped under the barbed wire. John Pentney, the secretary of the Thomas Hardy Society, is unlikely to forget being on those cliffs in pre-access days when a series of shells came whistling overhead.

The military role of the Royal Armoured Corps' School at Lulworth Camp has been to turn out a hundred and fifty qualified tank gunners each year. Tyneham's northern heathland and West Holme Heath are used for training tank crews in the roughest of combat conditions and live firing is carried out from concrete-based firing points. Shells overshoot the Tyneham valley and drop in the English Channel; the fourteen mile sea danger zone extends well outside Britain's three miles of territorial waters.

Tanks operating inside the parish of Tyneham have done considerable damage at Povington but only armoured cars operate in the southern valley. Their closer-range fire is aimed at moving targets on the slope of Gad Cliff. Fulmars, shags and cormorants breed only a few hundred yards away on the sheer four hundred feet limestone crags.

Attitudes have changed since the ancient badger setts on the hills were bulldozed in 1967. Where, however, the military finds particular difficulty in cleaning up its act is that wire-guided missiles are as much part of anti-tank warfare in the 1990s as they were in the 1960s. Whereas I had assumed that they would evolve into sophisticated electronic and laser-guidance systems, wire remains favourite for the task because it is unjammable.

LAW 80 (Light Anti-tank Weapon, calibre 80 mm) is a

hand-held, shoulder-fired anti-tank missile with a range of half a mile. It leaves in its wake a length of wire that has a similar gauge and flexibility to nylon fishing line. Much more environment-unfriendly is the longer-range TOW version (Tube-launched Optically-guided Wire-controlled), which is launched from a stand or a vehicle, even a helicopter. It can be fired up to four miles; controlled by a bobbin of wire of this length.

In theory the trails of spent missile wire are recovered after each set of firings. In practice, however, for years the scrub of Tyneham valley has been engulfed by an insidious cats-cradle which is a menace for wildlife.

I have seen the head of a roe-buck with wire tangled around its antlers like cotton on the spool of a sewing machine. The military have mounted such horrific specimens as exhibits to get across the message that soldiers should clean up after themselves. That is easier said than done, once the wire has draped the sycamore trees and snagged and snapped into inaccessible lengths. "Intensive military training is by its very nature a destructive activity," a land agent admitted on one of the army's image-boosting conservation days.

Founding Tyneham Action Group, 1967

In the mid-1960s I decided to form a Tyneham Action Group and founded it with a "Surrender Purbeck" slogan, the campaign being launched in the first issue of Dorset County Magazine which was published in the first week of December 1967 (though dated "Spring 1968" to confuse newsagents into keeping it on sale longer; you have to be an optimist if you plant trees or start magazines). As I opened the resulting deluge of mail that outnumbered the Christmas cards that year I was instantly secretary of the nascent Tyneham Action Group and eventually of its successor bodies, the 1943 Committee and Friends of Tyneham, until a membership of two thousand slid to oblivion as the government pre-empted further campaigning with such attractive concessions on public access that there was no longer a mass movement. Some said it had been a meteoric rise, but meteors can only fall, and so it came to pass. In the wave of enthusiasm I booked the Moule Institute at Dorchester for a public meeting on 18 May 1968, and opened the proceedings with a fighting speech:

"Tyneham is devastated. Its cottages and farms are smashed by shellfire. Many of the evicted now lie in alien cemeteries, and the remainder have re-established their lives elsewhere. So a simple return and a genuine honouring of the pledge is no longer possible.

"Our answer must be to advocate that this superb stretch of five miles of the finest British coastline – from Lulworth Cove to Kimmeridge – is given to the National Trust. People have a right to visit it. Many have only heard of it from the lucky few who can remember Sunday picnics at Arish Mell, Mupe and Worbarrow during the Thirties."

Once you have a committee around you, and are holding torchlight processions and taking deputations to see Peter Carrington and petitions into Number Ten, the answers are no longer that simple. By the time of our first open meeting in hostile territory, at Wareham in November 1968, the ideals of that first meeting had been compromised. Both main points were trimmed. Firstly there were some who wanted to become agents of the former landowners and their families, dropping my point about the National Trust, and there was dissent about what we were fighting to release. They wanted it restricted to the coastal valley at Tyneham as that was regarded as a practical objective. Others did speak out at this, and I should have taken the advice of a strong-minded 65-year-old, Mr E. Nimmo of Shillingstone:

> The ultimate objective must be the re-opening of all this magnificent coast to public access. Until this is done, how can the proposed coastal footpath become a reality?
> Why should we accept that Arish Mell is lost for ever because there is an atomic waste pipe there? The fact is that the War Department should never have been allowed to establish themselves on this coast at all.

112

My sole reason for wishing to live to a hundred is that I might then see the army pushed off the Dorset coast.

I did make a stand on his points a year later and hijacked much of the membership to form an alternative pressure group. Had we avoided the pitfall of shallow consensus from the start the campaign might well have attained a momentum that was unstoppable.

Instead the resignations started. Committee member Carl Baker withdrew in protest that a single critic had been allowed to stampede the meeting into whitewashing the army:

> The "gnomes of Whitehall" cannot take the whole of the blame. They may have sent the army there, but they did not instruct them to place their targets where they would do most damage; they did not order them to let the grazing rights, causing so much unnecessary suffering to animals, nor to employ louts such as the one who murdered the badgers.
> Both Legg and I tried to bring out what seems to me a truer picture of the situation, but we were more or less disowned by the committee – so, too, was our guest speaker, who stressed how ironical it was that the army, which is supposed to defend our heritage, should now be destroying it.

'How painful it is to remember'

The campaign unleashed a torrent of nostalgia from former Tyneham people, now scattered across the world. Diana I.H. Muehsam of New Jersey spent her childhood with her grandfather, H.H. House, at South Tyneham Farm between 1933 and 1942. They moved into Kimmeridge vicarage a year before the eviction:

> A childhood in such beautiful, idyllic surroundings would be hard to describe here after all the time which has gone by, knowing the uselessness of looking back. How painful it is to remember the small warm pools at Charnel where first I learned to swim, the "winkles" we cooked in tins on the beach, the endless picnics, fishing, looking for crabs at Broad Bench. Then there was Old Sticky (Mr Stickland) the fisherman, who built the "Minnimoo" and taught us a game which we called after him, "Sticky's Game". The magnificent profile of Gad Cliff is something I should love to see again one day. There is so much to tell, that I better stop right here. It hurts too much.

Mrs Ethel Irene Horlock of Findley Place, Swanage, was born at Baltington Farm on 3 September 1890 and lived there and at Lutton until 1916. In 1973 she still hoped to return to Tyneham: "I was born there, baptised in the little church, also confirmed at that church, so naturally would like to visit it again, and see the graves of my relatives."

'The postman found us by our names'

Mrs Annie Elizabeth Lowman came to Tyneham at the age of ten in 1910 and lived there with her grandmother for five years: "My grandmother lived in the cottage by the brook which did not have name or number. The postman found us by our names. It applied to everyone. The house has now been blasted down from what I could see last summer, 1972. My ancestors lie at rest in the churchyard, in the name of Richards, an uncle and great-great grand-parents. They lie by the wall near the school, if it's still there. There should be two headstones. I will come to Tyneham again when the church is open. I want to clean the headstones if I can."

Gwendoline House, now Mrs Dicker, was born at Sear-ley's Living, Povington, on 18 September 1923 and later moved to North Egliston Farm, from where the family were evicted by the military in 1943. Her farmhouse on the heath was still standing in the 1970s, though without its windows.

Arthur Davies, who lived as a child between 1924 and 1936 in the first house on the right as you enter Tyneham village, recalled scratching his initials in the stable window at Tyneham Farm. He returned in 1972 and found it again. Phyllis Agnes May Farrington was the daughter of H.G. Green, the tenant of North Egliston Farm Cottages, and was born there on 9 May 1923. She wrote to me from Australia in 1973:

> Mrs Hurd was the proprietress of the store in the village. Mr Smith was the farmer. The little school was no longer being used in those days, much to my disappointment. We travelled

by bus to Corfe Castle. I often looked through the windows of Tyneham school. It looked so cosy, and more like a dolls' house compared with "the big school" at Corfe.

I remember the beautiful little church where I attended Sunday school, and the inscription outside by the water trough, which started off: "Whoever drinketh this water shall thirst again ... In my childlike way I believed that the water there was somehow different, and sure enough it was not long before I was thirsty again, whilst taking the long walk home.

Mrs Muriel Gould only lived at the Gardener's Cottage for two years at the start of the war but for her, like all the others, it was long enough for Tyneham to make its lasting impression: "Having only lived in Tyneham a short time, these are my memories, of working for the Bond family at Tyneham House, and helping out at Baltington Farm, for Mr Longman. There was the village hall where dances were held once a month, and the weekly trip on market days to Wareham, by Shearby's bus. I have the memory of my in-laws, whose understanding of the countryside thrilled me."

'Above all I wish to be interred there'

Mrs Gould's husband, Jack, was born at Tyneham on 24 October 1912 and was the vicarage gardener. Of all the former Tyneham residents he had the greatest determination to return: "I would love to return when the opportunity is offered, and above all I wish to be interred there when my time comes, if we get it back or not. The house where I was born has the roof off but the side walls are standing, the Gardener's Cottage is in much better shape. I have my grandparents on my mother's side buried at Tyneham, with my Uncle Tom." He remembers much about Tyneham life, though ironically he was fighting for his country in India when his home was seized:

Memories flood back of my childhood days at Tyneham. The small village school that held twenty-five to thirty children when full; it was also used as a village hall for a time, and therefore has a small stage. On school days the stage was curtained off and the children were taught by Miss Bright, in the main part of the school. The older children were under strict control of Mrs Pritchard, the headmistress. I, like many more, never liked school: but how grand those days were.

After school hours, I often used to go leading horses in the haymaking season; it is such fun in the country. One can always find plenty to do. One memory I shall never forget, I would be about four years old then. A cousin of mine, about the same age, was on holiday, staying with us. We were playing at the time, at the far end of the garden that overlooks the stream. I crawled into a large wooden water butt. I just went rolling down the sides of the steep banks of the stream through stinging nettles. I was none the worse, but for the stings.

On leaving school, I worked for the vicar, tending his garden, and in the summer evenings I fished in the bay. Many hours were spent talking to the fishermen, Jack Miller, and Tom Miller, on the wooden bench outside. Many a true tale they have told me. The walks I had with my parents, over the hill to East Lulworth, were on a Sunday evening after church. I have many times had to "pump" the organ from the time I left school until I joined the army in 1933.

No doubt to me about the church, this building is the jewel of the valley. I do sincerely hope the bells will sound, and people will pray in this lovely church, St Mary's.

My best memory was during the 1914-18 war, when my father was going back to the front from leave. I can picture him now bending over my cot to kiss me goodbye.

John Gould, old soldier of the Devonshire Regiment and retired Wareham roadman, lived in a council flat at Sandford, which he had named "Tyneham". The occupation of the village became the driving force of his later life, and the spur to many of us to troop his case, "flogging a dead horse" according to our Wareham detractors, through the corridors of power. Tyneham in retrospect was his total motivation: "It's always in my thoughts. My home will always be there. If I could, I would go back tomorrow. It is a wicked shame that the pledge hasn't been kept." Lord Fenner Brockway, the veteran socialist, accompanied him around Whitehall and the Houses of Parliament; an alien world where history had evolved differently.

On the northern side of the range of hills, where Luckford Lake issues from the overgrown hedgerows of Whiteway and Povington, was the largest and most orderly of the heathland communities and that with the longest history. Most of the small, irregular fields surrounding the hamlet of Povington were created in their present shapes before the Norman Conquest. Half a mile to the north of the chalk ridge, a rough road ran from East Lulworth to Creech Grange and linked tiny farmsteads that grew out of the mixed soils in the long, narrow belt below the hill. Somewhat fertile and watered by ample springs, the settlements were nonetheless constantly pressed from the north by the wide plain of desolation of the dreariest, most uneventful of the Dorset heaths.

The White homestead at Povington

To people like Mrs S.B. White, the thought of returning again to see her former home was too painful to be contemplated. Her mother's homestead on Povington Heath "can just boast a pile of stones, part of a chimney stack and a lonely and gruesome-looking yew tree". She recalled her grandparents for me, and their life at Povington, and this story of the end of one family of heathcroppers shows the disruption caused by the military occupation. It was recorded in 1970:

My mother lived in a little house called Whiteway. It seemed large to me when I was a child but I daresay it was really quite small. Whiteway lay almost in a line with the round, scooped out, hollow of chalk in the hillside.

I must have been very young when I was there with my mother, so my recollections are bitty. But I can remember it had a thatched roof and walls of that gritty mud substance; very thick with wide window sills. The large living room had a massive scrubbed table and an open fireplace with a mantelshelf along the top. Mother told of sitting on the stone slabs inside the fireplace, putting on fircones and roasting potatoes during the evenings. A large, black smokey kettle hung on a chain, and you could look up the centre of the chimney to see the sky. Apparently they used to sweep the chimney by letting a faggot of furze (*fuzz*, they called it) down on a stone.

Grandmother was a large, comfortable woman, with a soft singing voice. I only ever saw her with a black dress and enveloping white apron. She smiled a lot and worked very hard. I think she had fourteen children, although I believe some of them died at birth.

The family became very scattered: I think I still have an aunt in Canada, and an aged uncle at Poole. The grandparents could neither read nor write and my mother used to correspond with her two brothers who went to the 1914-18 war. She was forced to convey the news that they were both killed in the battles in France. I remember a garden with a stream, and lots of outbuildings with chickens and a few cows. There was also a little house down the garden with numerous horseshoes on the lintel of the door and a double-seated lavatory. Mother spoke of having to scrub the seats until they were gleaming white wood. She also told of going up to the chalkpit to clean the knives.

They apparently also had bees. I was always interested in the tales about them, and heard fascinating stories of Grandma telling her bees all family news, both good and bad. Mother often had to go and listen to hear if the bees were singing and if the queen was calling. One of the younger girls, Edith, worked at Tyneham House. She married but her husband was also killed in the war and she was left with a little boy. Later she died and was always discussed in grim whispers (galloping consumption and a broken heart) but Gerald was brought up by another aunt at Hollow Ditch, a smallholding north-west of Creech Grange. I spent many happy holidays with them and am more familiar with that part.

This was a sturdy little house with little windows and thick walls. Large cupboards by the fireplace housed hams and smoked bacon. Breakfasts there were marvellous meals — my aunt and uncle having done hours of work fetching the cows and milking by hand, had by this time developed large appetites. Hence we had masses of eggs, thick slices of bacon and chitterlings and soft potato cakes. Sometimes they cooked eels which cousin Gerald had teased me with early in the morning.

Mother's name was Beatrice Bessie Balson, and you can imagine how she was teased about that. Her sister, Susan, who lived at Hollow Ditch, married Matthew Charles. Grandfather Balson worked at Tyneham House. He had very bright, blue eyes and I remember I was a little in awe of him. He was such a silent, gnome-like figure with his white beard and sideburns.

Little things drift back as I try to recollect. I can remember singing around the old harmonium, which we eventually had in our home, and many times I wept whilst mother sang and laboriously played sad songs. Her mother had taught her songs about little Mary dying, becoming an angel, and similar sad laments — always most tragic, but I suppose it was a pleasure for them.

At Hollow Ditch there was a large russet apple tree, large wooden butter-pats with intricate patterns, and rows of lovely golden butter laid on a tray ready to go to Wareham market. Once a lady named Elsie Cake called on a straight-up, no nonsense bicycle with a fancy chain-guard. She hopped off in a most graceful manner, in spite of long skirts and button boots. I later tried to do the same but came a cropper. In the evenings, I would go across the heath to Marepool and watch the deer drinking at dusk. It was also from this spot that I watched Lulworth Castle burning [in 1929]. My grandparents are buried at Tyneham churchyard but Aunt Susan was buried at Steeple. She ended her days in a cottage at Kimmeridge, having heen moved there at the time of the evacuation. But she always hoped to return to Hollow Ditch ...

Alms Grove and the other lost commons

The last echoes of the way of life of the heathcroppers and Purbeck's poorer folk were heard at a series of common land registration inquiries in the 1970s into ancient rights. There was no shortage of documentary evidence that the customary usage of the heath had been formerly widespread and accepted but the question was whether these rights had lapsed into extinction. Mrs Mavis Caver of Morden was involved in the registration of thousands of acres. She explained at numerous hearings that the heath was used as a communal resource by the cottagers who turned their cattle on to it, collected furze for ovens, dug great stacks of peat from it each year, and used heather to roof outhouses. The heathcroppers sited hundreds of bee-hives across the heath and produced the best honey in Dorset.

In the great bulk of cases the rights fell through lack of living verification – the law had come too late. As an example of the vast scale of the rights that have been lost there was firm proof in the archives that common rights existed across more than three thousand acres in the Purbeck tank gunnery ranges alone. There the Ramblers Association registered Povington Heath (770 acres); West Holme Heath (314 acres); Holme Heath (443 acres); Grange Heath (646 acres); Coombe Heath (327 acres);

Lulworth Heath (121 acres). I also registered Alms Grove – its very name implying charity for the poor – at the turn-off into Tyneham Valley, and another four hundred acres below the north side of the hill. As the area had been compulsorily depopulated there was no case that could be sustained. It had been hoped by those making the registrations that the ancient rights of common might one day be transformed into the modern privilege of public access for air and exercise.

Hot pursuit of trespassing MP

The most bizarre trespassing adventure to take place inside the Lulworth Ranges happened on the sunny morning of Sunday 15 April 1973 when a Member of Parliament, his agent, and myself were chased three miles across downland, along a stream bed and through woodland by twelve soldiers and three Landrovers. The entire Tyneham valley was sealed off to the public at that time but though we were out of condition we kept giving our pursuers the slip and left in our own time.

Graham Tope, the member for Sutton and Cheam, had been staying at the Dorset cottage of his agent Michael Key. Michael and I decided to give Graham a walk in Dorset's wild country. It started ordinarily enough along the ridgeway from Whiteway Hill to Flower's Barrow, where we stood in silhouette looking down over Lulworth Camp and the coast. From there we stumbled and slid down the smooth grass, on our backsides, towards Worbar-row.

After we had descended three hundred feet to the ruins of an old stone barn we saw there was a problem. Two soldiers were watching us through fieldglasses from a Landrover parked near the beach.

So we changed course and turned away from the sea, along the bramble thickets that skirt the foot of the escarpment to Baltington, half a mile away. Here I took photographs, until Michael said: "Come on Rodney, there's

120

another Landrover coming down from Whiteway." Re-inforcements had been radioed from Lulworth. I continued to squint into the viewfinder and could see nothing except the farm. When Michael told me to hurry I looked up to see that there was a cloud of dust approaching and I had given the vehicle a few hundred yards additional advantage. The three of us ran due south, past the dark green corpse of a Saladin armoured car, tangling our feet in the lines of discarded white wire from manually-guided missiles. A pair of roe deer jumped out of the bushes, with heart-shaped white tufts gleaming from their rumps.

In the trees of Tyneham Gwyle we found a deep-cut bend in the stream bed and lay still, watching the water rippling between the stones, for fifteen minutes. All was then silent so we moved off, again changing direction and this time following the stream up the valley. For four hundred yards we crashed, staggered and fell through the trees which were strewn with thirty years of uncleared deadwood. We then boldly decided to break out across the open ground on the south side of the Tyneham-Worbarrow track to climb the slopes of Gad Cliff. Just as we were poised to climb the barbed wire fence at the roadside a jeep appeared, coming up from the bay.

We jumped backwards and flung our faces in the stinking wild garlic that smothered the ground. The truck was so close that as it rumbled by I was able to hear one of the men say: "We've lost the bastards."

Immediately it disappeared around the bend we leapt across the fence, ducked under the wire on the other side of the road and ran south, bounding madly uphill for a few hundred yards in full view of the entire Tyneham valley. Michael led the way in an Olympic sprint that seemed quite likely to launch him off the clifftop, but Graham and I strained and pained and then forced ourselves up the last few paces to the cover of an old stone wall.

None of us had looked back, but we were sure that we must have been spotted and that the fit professionals would be hurtling towards us with a speed that would make our uphill run seem feeble. As we were in no state to run any further we slumped back against the wall and prepared to give up.

Then as life returned to our bodies we scanned the valley and were amazed to see a party searching the Baltington brambles where we had been more than half an hour before. They were a mile away, and all had been looking downwards as we made our uphill flight in full view. Confidence brimmed and we saw ourselves in the next television remake of Colditz. We lay back in smug self-congratulation in the sun, expecting to resume our walk in peace when the soldiers had disappeared.

Instead a Landrover hurtled towards us in full cry, sweeping its path through the deep grass of the ungrazed hillside. Our stone wall was exposed from the side so we bolted round the back of a blackberry bush and repeated our tactic of lying silent. They passed by, in what must have been only a chance sweep.

The moment they were gone we ran uphill, in and out of view, for half a mile to the slopes of Tyneham Cap. We could see one Landrover searching Worbarrow and another with four men who started to look under everything in the Rectory grounds, the best part of a mile away. The sound of a third Landrover came from Tyneham village and they obviously thought we had moved only a few hundred yards from Baltington and were hiding in one of the ruined buildings in the valley. We reviewed the entire manoeuvres from a five-hundred foot hilltop.

Next we changed direction through ninety degrees for the sixth time since the chase began, noisily descending through a belt of sycamore, beech and primrose woods to the ruins of Tyneham House, confident that the adversaries were making so many sounds of their own that they would never hear us. The house was as it had been left after demolition in 1968 but we were surprised to find that at the back, in the older servants' quarters, workmen from the Department of the Environment had spent the previous week supporting ceilings, fitting doors and repairing masonry. The original mediaeval wing of Tyneham House was being restored whilst the ranges were still being used for tank gunnery; the "impossibility" that was given in 1968 as the excuse for demolition. We were elated as we took it as a physical sign that Tyneham was to be free.

From here, at our own pace, we walked and rested in a northward saunter to the upper reaches of Tyneham's *gwyle* stream, through the sheep fields, and then directly up the steep side of the Purbeck Hills. We watched the Landrovers pull out along the road and left the military barbed wire at Povington Hill viewpoint, two minutes after a car had arrived there to take us to lunch at the Weld Arms in East Lulworth.

From there I telephoned the Range Office to tell them they could stop looking for us — but there was no reply, as they were all still doing just that.

Monica Hutchings and 'The Fight for Tyneham', 1968

For the benefit of those who venture into the research of the Tyneham cause célèbre I would point out that although I edited "The Fight for Tyneham" in the summer of 1968 and added its by-lined introduction I did not write the main text of the booklet. This was produced with commendable speed and enthusiasm by Church Knowle novelist Monica Hutchings. She insisted that it would carry more weight by being anonymously attributed to a committee. Anyone who has ever served on a committee will realise the inherent contradiction.

In the rush a series of minor errors slipped into the quoted material, so the few bits that are included here have been checked against original documents to ensure that this time they are word perfect. I have also tended to quote more fully from originals, resulting sometimes in a change of emphasis, and I have put together the full story of Lulworth and Povington whereas the sole intention of the original booklet was to make a strong propaganda case for the release of just Tyneham Valley.

Monica had the *bottle* – as the squaddies say – to tour her Tyneham slide show through what must have seemed like a thousand nights with the Women's Institutes of the West, and had overcome breast cancer, but was losing the wider battle for her health. She could not adjust to failing sight in the mid-1970s and was to swim to her death off Argyll.

Tyneham feudalism, 1769-style

One consolation in failure was that a revived Tyneham, in a Purbeck mauled by intensive agriculture and maintaining prime prices for second homes, could not have reverted to the 1930s idyll. Then it would not have been unique, but the other lost communities lack the precise cut-off and have evolved into something completely different that we recognise as normal rural living in the latter quarter of the twentieth century.

A substantial number of people suggested that it was a benefit, a liberation, that Tyneham's intensely feudal paternalism had been ended. Their objection would have been even stronger if a black marble inscription in the north wall of the church at Tyneham had then been on public view:

> Near this Place lye ye Body of Elizabeth Tarrant *Servant* to Mrs Bond of Tineham which Station *she* continued 34 years.
> To ye Memory of *her Prudence Honesfty and Induftry*, this Monument is erected. *She* died *Auguft ye 2nd* 1769 in *ye* 54 Year of her Age.

Miss L.M.G. Bond's *Tyneham* which enchanted many, with the closed world of country estate living, struck others as a study in slavery. The system relied upon evictions when people were no longer regarded as useful, and its illusory tranquillity depended upon a humiliating degree of compliance. Some had detailed memories that cancelled out the past virtues that villagers were so eager to impart. Several old people, reacting to a leaflet thrust into their hands, said that in the 1930s Farmer Smith would lock the gate to close the mile-long track to Worbarrow beach, and anyone wanting to take the matter further could do so with a bull.

Runaway Hercules blew-up off Purbeck, 1969

An advanced radar drama exploded off the Purbeck coast in May 1969, though what happened is still largely supposition. It concerns the occasional tradition throughout the American forces of suicidal misappropriation of military hardware. A ground staff officer, Sergeant Paul Meyer of the United States Air Force, had stolen a 30 ton Lockheed C130 Hercules transporter – one of the last generation of heavy military turbo-props – from Mildenhall airbase in East Anglia. He flew the plane single-handed southwards through the busiest air lanes in the world, and vanished.

Defence and ground-control radar systems failed to follow the movements of one of the largest and slowest military aircraft. The Daily Express reported that the Hercules "made a hole in Britain's delicate radar system" – for the technically bizarre reason that "the plane was going out, not coming in". Three weeks later there was a statement in Parliament that the plane had been "continuously tracked by British radar".

The fact was that Paul Meyer flew over the River Thames and across Kent on automatic pilot, with Mildenhall's control centre only able to register his position when Meyer spoke to them on his radio. Some claimed the Hercules was invisible to radar as it carried the latest package of electronics for absorbing radar waves and preventing them from being reflected back to the ground.

Meyer was talked into turning right down the entire length of the English Channel, which had the advantages of preventing his ploughing into a built-up area and also lessening the chances of mid-air collision. As he flew off the Lizard he was hooked up to his wife via the radio network and she, in a desperate early morning phone call, tried to talk him into flying the plane back to a British airfield.

Meyer carried out a U-turn over the Scilly Isles and crossed Devon to Lyme Bay. Now, having a working conversation going, it seems unlikely his base commanders wanted to risk the disaster that could accompany an attempted landing. While an officer who knows the equipment can fly a Hercules without that much difficulty, it is another matter to put the thing back on the ground. The smooth-talking continued, and Meyer was asked to locate various knobs and panels, presumably as a dry-run of the landing techniques.

In the process it seems he may have touched a red lever the purpose of which he was unaware. It was the "destructor", though his superiors would hardly have called it that over the radio. Anyway, the story of the runaway Hercules ended about 40 miles south of Lulworth Cove at 4 a.m. on Friday 23 May 1969. Paul Meyer and his plane blew up.

Western security could relax. There was even a convenient explanation for those at Mildenhall – to suggest Meyer had simply tried to ditch in the sea. Said a spokesman: "It takes a highly trained and skilled pilot to land on the sea. There's a strong possibility the plane broke up."

The biggest hole in Dorset

Much of the ball clay produced from open workings in Purbeck in the early 1970s was taken from a pit of breathtaking proportions. It was secret and operating without planning permission until I announced the existence of "the biggest hole in Dorset" in issue 31 of Dorset County Magazine and seized the front page lead story in the Bournemouth Evening Echo. The pit was a closely guarded secret discovered only by a few who have penetrated as trespassers deep into the permanent no-go interior of the Lulworth tank gunnery ranges. Between Povington Wood and the sliced remains of a heathland knoll known as Raymond's Firs is the largest hole in Dorset. I wrote:

"It is a quarter-mile across, 75 feet deep, and still growing. Towering cliffs of soft sands – all colours from yellow, brown and orange through to purple – girdle a crater that opens out of the heart of a complex of ancient hedges perpetuating the original field boundaries of the Saxon hamlet of Povington. The gargantuan hole is in the shadow of the Purbeck Hills, just over a mile west from Creech Grange.

"Three men and a crane are little more than specks at the bottom of this new world as they hack into sixteen solid feet of grey ball clay. The workface is worth £10 a ton. Through the day and night the pit is protected by the constant running of a pump which sucks at lines of muddy pools and prevents English China Clays' biggest open-pit spectacle in Dorset from turning into a great lake.

"Ball clay extraction has carried on continuously inside the Lulworth ranges since the entire area was depopulated by the military takeover of 1943. Unnoticed, the crane and men have been able to gobble a hole that is beyond description. Such a pit on Arne would make the Poole Harbour shoreline resemble Sinai after nuclear attack.

"In contrast, a short distance away from the pit – between the hole and farm buildings at West Creech – stands the rotting wooden headgear of a disused underground mine. The vertical shaft has filled with clay and old railway sleepers. It is surrounded by marshy ponds and the living ecosystem of ground that has been able to adjust to a more gentle method of mining.

"It was this mine that betrayed the existence of its modern counterpart. In May 1973 a group of industrial archaeologists traced the line of the former Pike Bros' clay railway from Furzebrook to its western limit inside the 'Danger, Unexploded Shells' notices here on the fields of Povington. They mapped the shapes of long abandoned waste heaps and then stood in amazement at the top of a precipice. 'Kimberley must be like this,' one of them told us by phone the next morning. 'You could drop the Blue Pool in there several times over.'

"The man-made hole is where there used to be virtually level land. It owes its environmental acceptibility to a unique private existence possible only because the Ministry of Defence's red death-warning signs have kept away all prying eyes until the archaeologists and ourselves intruded.

"Clay working at West Creech took place before the war on land owned by the Bond family of Creech Grange. In 1952 the freehold of the land was compulsorily purchased by its occupiers, the War Department. (The late) Lieutenant-Colonel Ashley Bond, representing Pike Bros, Fayle and Cooper, questioned Government solicitor J.R. Turner about the future of the clayfield at a public inquiry in 1961. The subject of the inquiry was the stopping-up of 96 miles of public highways running through the Lulworth ranges. Bond: 'You know, Sir, that we have rights under lease to work out in this area. I take it you are not in any way proposing to interfere with this or the access to it, are you?' 'They remain unimpaired.' 'Thank you very much.'"

Dorset County Council later issued retrospective planning permission to legalise the hole, twenty years after its digging had commenced.

Military ecology, 1971

The most effective backlash against the Tyneham campaign came from naturalists and army officers who suddenly proclaimed the virtues of military ecology. General Sir John Hackett told radio listeners to "This Island Now" in May 1971 that it was positively beneficial for the wildlife if the land were held by the army, the prime example being Salisbury Plain, the largest area of natural downland turf in the British Isles:

> The great enemy to wildlife is not bangs and shells and things like that but people. You quite often find the nesting places of rare birds in this country in the impact area on firing ranges, not at the firing points but in the impact area where there is very, very rare disturbance by man. It's safe to say that if the training areas which are now kept at a very low-population level were opened up to the public, there are species of wildlife in England now which would become rarer and some which would certainly become extinct. Scrubland is absolutely essential to the continuance of many types of wildlife but scrubland is a very uneconomic form of land in terms of land use, and but for the military, scrubland would probably disappear in the United Kingdom.

Much is made now of the credit side to the story. With the army in occupation, Tyneham's wilderness conditions have turned the land into a vast nature reserve. It has an immense reservoir of wildlife and is restocking much of civilian-held south-east Dorset with animals and birds. There is a greater concentration of wildlife inside the Lulworth East Holme Ranges than in any of Dorset's official nature reserves.

It is one of the more welcome side effects of military occupation but it must not be thrown away one day by the misguided enthusiasm of those who can only appreciate countryside that has been devastated by the methods of modern farming. Tyneham is different from the rest of Dorset only because it has never been farmed intensively, and it must remain that way. Thanks to the army, Tyneham has become the greatest natural wilderness on this side of Dartmoor, which makes it unique in lowland England. The peregrine falcon, one of our largest birds of prey, still breeds inside the uncultivated vastness of the Lulworth tank gunnery ranges.

Not only the wildlife has been saved. Tyneham also has three virtually complete mediaeval field systems and the remains of the banks and hedges of Saxon landholdings. Plough ridges have survived at Tyneham from the thir-teenth century. They were cut at the time when the parish church was built. Nowhere else in the whole of Dorset have such remains been so perfectly preserved. As historian Christopher Taylor has commented: "Without the army to protect them, these remains would have been ploughed to extinction many years ago."

Two hundred acres of mediaeval cultivation strips survive under the rough pasture in Tyneham valley. The main area extends from the foot of the Purbeck Hills at Whiteway Hill (Ordnance Survey map reference SY 880 808) in a broad sweep southwards, either side of Rook Grove and then across the whole area between Tyneham village and Tyneham House, and finally upwards on the inland slopes of Gad Cliff to within one field of the edge.

The other great cluster stretches from north-west of North Egliston (SY 897 810) and southwards beside the parish boundary with Steeple all the way to the cliffs at Charnel (SY 902 791). Westwards it spreads beyond South Egliston to lynchets on Tyneham Cap (SY 891 797) and southwards down over most of the gently sloping coastal plain to the hinterland of Broad Bench at Stickland's Cottage (SY 898 792).

There are also several mediaeval hamlets in Tyneham parish which are virtually lost, having shrunken to single farmsteads. An extensive series of such settlement remains is east and south of North Egliston and includes a Chapel Close (SY 895 806). Tyneham village itself formerly covered a much greater area, having cottages and closes across what is now the car-park on both sides of the track between it and Tyneham Farm (SY 883 801). Likewise there was a cluster of habitations south and south-east of Baltington Farm (SY 877 804), including a cross-roads of tracks and another arm forked to give access on to the western open field.

Crichel Down rules
would prevent tenants' return

The Tyneham campaign finally crumbled because Government ministers of both main parties and high-ranking civil servants had made it clear that if any part of the Lulworth ranges were relinquished from state ownership it would be offered under the so-called Crichel Down rules to the former landowners and their descendants. On the other hand there would be no right of return for any of the displaced tenants or their families, who formed the bulk of the dispossessed. The pledge would remain dishonoured.

Neither was the principal eastern landowner-in-succession, Major-General Mark Bond, taken with our plans to have most of the area left as a wilderness; he told Lord Brockway that he opposed the nature reserve proposals and saw himself as a kind of middleman landlord-steward. General Bond had written to me from the headquarters of 12 Infantry Brigade on 2 May 1968 to "keep the facts straight", making it clear that he had it in writing from the Ministry of Defence that "in the hypothetical case of the handing back of Tyneham the land would have to be offered first to you and the other owners [successors] at the time of acquisition".

The campaign to bring about a transfer to the National Trust went as far as a deputation to see their director general in his Queen Anne's Gate boardroom in London, leaving with assurances that they would respond enthusias-

tically if it did come their way. I should have realised from Mark Bond's helpful and factual analysis that our stand was presumptuous and flawed. I now feel that the release of the land would have unleashed more problems than it solved, and shudder sometimes at the thought of how close we came to an illusory success. The compromise that won the day at least gives everyone something.

The challenge eventually is to solve the contradiction of how we can conserve extensive wilderness areas without having to fire shells and missiles across them. Then the legal niceties can be faced, to achieve a formula for the substitution of more benign forms of national care, without the danger of the land concerned having to be passed back into private ownership.

'Jeff 'n Ange' – their stone seat, 1976

One contemporary improvement has been in the spirit of the old Tyneham. Below Tyneham Cap, on the west side, a warm and sheltered niche in the stone wall has been turned into a seat, with the credit line in the concrete reading "1976 J.M.: Jeff 'n Ange", plus what looks to be the footprint of their dog. It faces towards St Alban's Head, and walkers collapse into it each weekend, well aware that they are being treated to one of the best views in the British Isles.

The events of 1943 may well turn out to have been, in retrospect, a beneficial accident as they have created a remarkable natural oasis midway along the busy South Coast. It is up to us to ensure that this beauty is protected.

Demo outside gun range

A **BIT** of "minor harassment of the Army" was how Tyneham 1943 Committee chairman, Mr. Rodney Legg, described the group's hour-long demonstration at one of the gates to the Lulworth gunnery range yesterday.

The group are campaigning for the 7,200-acre range to be given up by the Army and handed over to the National Trust and a dozen members staged their sit-in at a gate on the Steeple to Lulworth road.

A couple of soldiers arrived in a Land Rover but seeing the group decided not to try to enter the range.

BY-LAWS

"After all, the Army closed the road so why should they go through the gate themselves," said Mr. Legg.

The group were protesting against new by-laws proposed for the range by the Ministry of Defence. The by-laws, if approved, would make it an offence punishable by a £20 fine to trespass on the range.

Say the group in their objection to the by-laws, "The fact is that no person, cow, deer, horse, sheep or tank has ever been blown up accidentally on the range. The by-laws are based on a confidence trick and there is no more danger in walking across the Lulworth range when firing is not taking place, than there is in using a pedestrian crossing. No-one would be fool enough to trespass on the range when firing is actually taking place."

The Daily Telegraph

RAMBLER PLAN WAL ON RANGI

By HUGH FERGUSO
Environment Correspor

HUNDREDS of wal
are planning a protest ramble across A firing-ranges at Lulwo Dorset, if Lord Carring Defence Secretary, dec to enforce proposed by-l against trespass.

They would defy barbed and red "Danger, unexpl shells" notices in the lon puted 1,700-acre area used the Royal Armoured Corps

The by-laws would en N C Os and higher ranks detain offenders instead merely asking them to le and would empower magistra to impose fines of up to £20

Closing date for objections next Monday.

No one blown up

Mr Rodney Legg, secretary the 1,000-strong 1943 Committ which campaigns for the Arm to restore the land to pub use, said yesterday that the pr test would be held before th enforcement date. He added "No person or animal has eve been blown up accidentally o the ranges. The by-laws ar based on a confidence trick."

A Ministry of Defence spokes man said that the by-laws were intended to safeguard the public. He emphasised that they had been approved in draft form already by Warcham and Pur heck rural council and Dorset nty Council.

TIMES — HERALD SERIES, WEEK ENDING SEPTEMBER 2, 1972

DANGER EXPLODED SHELLS KEEP OUT

Kenneth Allsop, Rodney Legg, John Gould, and Mrs. Mavis Caver, 1943 committee chairman, at Monday's rally.

20

They'll walk to challenge anges h

by the Americ exploration Powerstock. co But it was the a pation of Tyneha coastal strip that most of the speak rally, organised by t Committee.

Tyneham was chose plained chairman of the Dorset magazine, of the rally Rodney Legg, editor "it is at the heart of t Ministry of Defence's tank gunnery ranges, which were occupied by the army in 1943 with the promise of re-lease after the war."

Before Kenneth Allsop spoke the loudspeaker failed and there was a break of ten minutes for the public address to function again. Mr. Legg said: "The army have mains electricity down here but they won't let us use it."

This gave an opportunity for hecklers to catcall and one of them questioned the presence of landowners Richard Ryder and Michael Pitt Rivers. "I'm surprised you haven't got Admiral Drax," said one.

"He's dead," pointed out Mr. Legg.

Miss Helen Brotherton's reply to Mr. Allsop's attack on Dorset Naturalists Trust appears on page 9.

18 EVENING ECHO, BOURNEMOUTH, Wed., August 23, 1972

'Outrageous bombardment' of ancient monuments condemned at Tyneham

THE Ministry of Defence have now admitted the 1943 Committee's claim that four prehistoric burial mounds, scheduled as ancient monuments, have been destroyed by Army gunfire at Tyneham.

This admission is claimed by the Committee in their August newsletter, in which they announce that television interviewer and author Kenneth Allsop will be the principal speaker at neham car park at 3 next Holiday, August

ing are round barrows on heathland at Bovington in the parish of Tyneham. They will be excavated to see if any of their burials are still intact.

According to the committee's newsletter the Ministry say that the mounds have sustained accidental damage from time to time during the past 30 years.

"This I am afraid is unaval able unless we ca fit ing in the ar Under-Secret frey M witto Joh

theme of the rally is Protect the Dorset Area Beauty," and many local countryside pressure groups are taking part. Tyneham was chosen because it is at the heart of the Lul Ministry of Defence's tan worth tank gunnery range which were occupied by the Army in 1943 with the promise of re-lease at the end of the The 19

Mor recruits for Tyneham campaign

us hope we

127

WHY PROTESTERS WANT THE ARMY OUT OF BEAUTY SPOT

MORNING STAR Friday August 25 1972

This is all that is left of fishermen's cottages in Worbarrow Bay, Dorset, one of the loveliest stretches of coastline in southern England and officially designated an Area of Outstanding Natural Beauty.

Shattered by shellfire, as is the rest of the hamlet of Warbarrow, they lie within the Ministry of Defence's Lulworth tank gunnery range.

In Tyneham carpark at 3 p.m. on Bank Holiday Monday there is to be a protest rally in which many local countryside conservation pressure groups will take part.

One of them is The 1943 Committee, so-called because the Army occupied the area in 1943 with a promise to release it after the war. The Ministry has admitted that four prehistoric burial mounds, scheduled as ancient monuments, have been destroyed by firing.

On sale at the committee's stall (below) will be the first set of photographs taken inside a British Army battle range and published as postcards — four of them taken by photographers who trespassed behind barbed wire and read "Unexploded shells can kill you" notices.

They show the ruins of Tyneham House and the rectory, an upturned Churchill tank and the ruins of the parish church.

The 1943 COMMITTEE.

John Gould was born at TYNEHAM 60 YEARS AGO
HE WANTS TO COME HOME

JOIN US HERE

HONOUR THE PLEDGE OF CHURCHILL'S CABINET and RELEASE THIS LAND

Army to stay

WESTERN DAILY PRESS, Friday, October 13, 1972

CLAIMS that the Government was about to release the Lulworth tank gunnery ranges in Dorset, were denied last night by the Ministry of Defence.

The claims were made by Dorset Magazine editor Mr. Rodney Legg in an issue out yesterday. He is also secretary of the 1943 committee, which has been fighting for the release of the land.

Mr. Legg said the Army finally planned to honour its 27-year-old pledge to surrender the ghost village of Tyneham and more than 7,000 acres of Dorset coastland surrounding it, taken over as a training ground during the last war.

Mr. Legg said high-ranking army officers knew a Government statement concerning the move would be made soon.

A Defence spokesman claims

Army accused of shooting up history

By HARVEY ELLIOTT
Environment Reporter

FOUR ancient burial mounds on an Army firing range have been badly damaged.

And yesterday it was alleged that marker posts put up over the mounds to show tank gunners where **not** to fire were mistaken for targets.

The mounds — Bronze Age barrows — on the Dorset coast near Lulworth were taken over with about 6,000 acres by the Army in 1943.

Mr Rodney Legg, who is leading a campaign to have the whole area handed over to the National Trust, said yesterday: 'I was looking through binoculars towards the spot where the barrows should be. There was nothing there but shell holes and tank tracks. It was horrible.'

He complained to his MP, Mr Evelyn King (Tory, South Dorset) who has asked the Defence Minister to look into the matter.

Meanwhile, Department of the Environment officials have inspected the barrows, found four of them badly damaged and recommended their excavation.

The barrows have remained untouched, until now, for 3,500 years.

Mr Legg said: 'The Army had managed to avoid the barrows completely.

'Then they decided to put up marker posts to show gunners exactly where the spots to avoid were.

'These are metal stars mounted on posts and it seems to me that somehow they mistook the signs for targets and just opened fire.'

Daily Mail, Thursday, March 30, 197_

THE RECTORY, TYNEHAM

Below: **Tailpiece shot of the ruin of the Rectory. The last rector, Rev Humphrey Churchill Money, was evicted along with his parishioners, six days before Christmas in 1943. Empty but intact for two decades, the building was first gutted by a dramatic fire – blamed on arsonists – and then reduced to a single storey by the Army. From the south-east. 1992.**

Photograph: Rodney Legg

The photographs on the cards were taken by two men who risked death from unexploded shells around the village.

The postcards show buildings in Tyneham which have not been seen by local residents since it was taken over by the Army 27 years ago; the ruins of Tyneham house, the derelict rectory and the parish church.

Ignored notices

Mr Rodney Legg, secretary of the 1943 Committee, the organisation fighting for the land's return to public use, said he and another photographer ignored the warning notices, "Danger Keep Out, Unexploded Shells Can Kill," and crossed barbed wire in order to take the photographs.

"They show people the areas where they are not allowed to go and are the best evidence we have got to make people indignant. There are over 7,000 acres of natural beauty where the public cannot go.

Limited sections of the area are opened during August.

On Sunday a campaign organised rally at T...

The Daily Telegraph, Wednesday, August 23, 1972

128

Protestors risk shells in ghost village

By TELEGRAPH REPORTER